the unofficial official handbook of good deeds

the unofficial official handbook of good deeds

YOUR
PICTURE HERE

NAME
_____
DATE OF BIRTH
_____

CELL
_____
E-MAIL
_____

ADDRESS
_____
_____
_____
_____
_____

SCHOOL
_____
_____
_____
_____
_____

FRIENDS
_____
_____
_____
_____
_____

PICTURE OF
HOME HERE

SCHOOL
PICTURE HERE

GROUP PICTURE
OF FRIENDS
HERE

FAVORITE MOVIES

1. _____
2. _____
3. _____
4. _____
5. _____

FAVORITE TV SHOW

1. _____
2. _____
3. _____
4. _____
5. _____

FAVORITE BANDS

1. _____
2. _____
3. _____
4. _____
5. _____

BEST DEED?

_____
_____
_____
_____
_____

FAVORITE PLACE

_____
_____
_____
_____
_____

FRIENDS' BIRTHDAYS

_____
_____
_____
_____
_____

FAVORITE
PICTURE HERE

FAVORITE
PICTURE HERE

FAVORITE
PICTURE HERE

THIS IS HOW IT WORKS

There are over 300 deeds in this book. So, whenever you feel a good deed coming on, pick one and check it off. Some deeds will need a little planning, so always think ahead, especially if it involves other people. Keep a positive attitude and you can make a world of difference—yes you can.

ICONS

When you've done a good deed, dude, let everybody know. Some will be green deeds, while others will be for individuals and the community.

CERTIFICATES

If you don't want to cut up your book, copy or scan the certificates, so they can be used over and over. That way you can enlarge them as well.

A RESOLUTION

I, the undersigned, being of sound body and mind, well, sort of, do hereby and henceforth resolve to do a good deed every day for an entire week. I, the undersigned, do promise to fulfil this resolution to the very best of my abilities. I, the undersigned, understand that this is an obligation to help create a nicer world.

Signed: Date:

DONE A DEED? CHECK IT OFF!

DEEDS

No doubt about it, deeds are not all the same! Some are harder than others. And they involve different numbers of people, too.

Easy   Medium   Advanced

Solo deed   Group deed

POWER UP THIS DEED

DO IT!

Mailing a postcard could be a good deed in itself—a flower picture which could have a message for mom on Mother's Day, perhaps.

COPY IT
FOLD IT
CUT IT

CAN

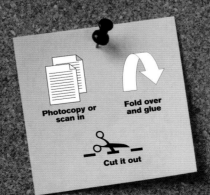

Photocopy or scan in

Fold over and glue

Cut it out

LONDON, NEW YORK, MUNICH,
MELBOURNE, DELHI

Text written by
L.L. Buller

Project Art Editor

Lee55

Editorial Lead
Heather Jones

DTP Designer
David McDonald

Production Editor
Kavita Varma

Senior Production Controller
Rachel Lloyd

Associate Publisher
Nigel Duffield

First American Edition, 2011
Published in the United States by DK Publishing, Inc. 375 Hudson Street,
New York, New York 10014

07 08 09 10 11 10 9 8 7 6 5 4 3 2 1

Copyright © 2011 Dorling Kindersley Limited

Boy Scouts of America ® is a registered trademark of the Boy Scouts of America. Printed under license
from Boy Scouts of America to DK Publishing. www.scouting.org

A Cataloging-in-Publication record for this book is available from the Library of Congress.

ISBN 978-0756-649890

DK books are available at special discounts for bulk purchases for sales promotions, premiums, fund-raising,
or educational use. For details, contact: DK Publishing Special Markets, 375 Hudson Street, New York, NY
10014 or SpecialSales@dk.com

Color reproduction by MDP, UK

Printed and bound in China by Hung Hing

Discover more at
www.dk.com

Boy Scouts of America
The mission of the Boys Scouts of America is to prepare young people to make ethical and moral
choices over their lifetimes by instilling in them the values of the Scout Oath and Law. The programs
of the Boy Scouts of America—Cub Scouting, Boy Scouting, Varsity Scouting, and Venturing—
pursue these aims through methods designed for the age and maturity of the participants.

Cub Scouting: A family- and home-centered program for boys in the first through fifth grade (or 7,
8, 9, and 10 years old). Cub Scouting's emphasis is on quality programs at the local level, where
the most boys and families are involved. Fourth- and fifth-grade (or 10-year-old) boys are called
Webelos (WE'll BE LOyal Scouts) and participate in more advanced activities that begin to prepare
them to become Boy Scouts.

Boy Scouting: A program for boys 11 through 17 designed to achieve the aims of Scouting through
a vigorous outdoor program and peer group leadership with the counsel of an adult Scoutmaster.
(Boys may also become Boy Scouts if they have earned the Arrow of Light Award or have
completed the fifth grade.)

Varsity Scouting: An active, exciting program for young men 14 through 17 built around five
program fields of emphasis: advancement, high adventure, personal development, service, and
special programs, and events.

Venturing: This is for young men and young women ages 14 through 20. It includes challenging
high-adventure activities, sports, and hobbies for teenagers that teach leadership skills, provide
opportunities to teach others, and to learn and grow in a supporting, caring, and fun environment.

For more information about Boy Scouts of America or its programs visit:

http://www.scouting.org

Boy Scouts of America®, the Universal Emblem, Boy Scouts™, Cub Scouts®, and rank insignia are
either registered trademarks or trademarks of the Boy Scouts of America in the United States and/
or other countries. Printed under license. All rights reserved.

GOOD DEEDS CHECKLIST

VISIT A LOCAL HOSPITAL, HOSPICE, OR NURSING HOME

Doing good deeds is about looking outside yourself, and deciding what you can do to make the world a better place. But you don't have to go around the world to share some happiness. Start in your own community, by paying a visit to a hospital, hospice, or nursing home. Volunteer to read or talk to people. Smile a lot. Be the kid in the room who listens. Take your friends along, if you like, and share the good deed–doing duties. You'll see how far a little bit of happiness can spread.

LEAVE A "GOOD-DEED TICKET" ON SOMEONE'S CAR

So, you're into this whole good-deed thing. (That's why you're reading this book, right?) If you get someone else to do something good, that's got to be a double good deed. So why not photocopy this good deed ticket (or create your own), fill it in, and leave it on someone's windshield to challenge them to do a good deed? They will probably be so happy not to get that **OTHER** kind of ticket, that they will be happy to share that happy feeling through a good turn. It would be almost a crime not to, right?

DGD MVD
DO NOT IGNORE

This **CITATION** is issued on the _____ day of the _____ year by the **DGD MVD**: Department of Good Deeds (Motor Vehicles Division). You have been **CHARGED** with the task of doing a really good deed today. If you do not act, you will be in **VIOLATION** of the **DGD MVD**. So, think of something FINE you can do for someone today. There will be no **PENALTY** if you decide not to do a good deed, but come on, try it! You might like it.

SIGNED

member of the **DGD OFFICE,**

YOUR CITY HERE

YOUR STATE HERE

www.dgdmvd.com

MAKING THE WORLD A BETTER PLACE SINCE YESTERDAY.

HELP DE-JUNK

GRIME SCENE—DO NOT ENTER

Your garage…what's in there, anyway? Go on, open the door and take a look into the murky depths. There's probably a car or truck or lawn mower in there, along with a few boxes full of something or other, a random shoe or two, a deflated basketball, a bunch of car stuff, a creaky ladder, some garden-y things, one slightly smelly tent, a few sticky cans of leftover house paint, a million of your old school papers, a couple of thingamagigs, and a whole stack of whatsits. When your garage starts to resemble a black hole that has sucked up all the matter around it, it is time to get to work. This is a challenging good deed, to say the least. Garages are big, and lots of that stuff ended up there because no one made the call whether to keep it or junk it. Still, get your family together on a non-rainy day and get to it. An organized garage is a happy garage.

WHAT YOU NEED:

Lots of garbage bags and clear plastic bags

Plenty of storage boxes in different sizes

Stick-on labels and a few black markers

Clean-up stuff: broom, dustpan, old towels, etc.

People power

THE GARAGE

GRIME SCENE—DO NOT ENTER

WHAT TO DO:

On the big day, wear old clothes—it's going to be dusty—and ask your parents to move the car out of the garage and park it on the driveway or street. Now move in. Pull everything out, and decide one of three things:

1 This is trash, it's broken and I can't fix it, and it's of no use to anyone. Put it right into a garbage bag.

2 This is not trash, and it's in good condition, but I don't want or need it anymore. Someone else, however, might really like to have this. Put it in a box for donation.

3 This is something I definitely want to keep. I use it all the time, or will use it in the future. Put it in an area for keepers.

Everything out of the garage and put in the right pile? Phew. (Did you find anything really surprising, like the Lost City of Atlantis?) Now you need to clean up the garage. Get busy with the broom and dustpan. If you have shelves, run an old towel over the surfaces to remove dust, spiderwebs, and other things you don't want to think about.

It's time to put the keeper stuff back in the garage. You may be a bit tired, but please don't just throw it back in and make another mess. Organize everything into groups: camping gear, sports stuff, tools, household bits and pieces, automotive supplies, general storage, and so on. Box up what you can box, and label it so it's easy to find. You can also put stuff in clear plastic bags so you can quickly see what it is.

Take the donation stuff to a charity thrift store (or call them for a pick-up) and take the garbage to the pick-up spot for collection.

Admire your tidy new garage and reward everyone for a deed well done.

CLEAN UP YOUR CLASSROOM

A cluttered classroom is distracting. When there is messy clutter on the desks, walls, and floor, it's harder to focus and learn. (Do you remember how clean and new everything felt on the first day of school, and how you felt ready to learn? Sort of?) Ask your whole class to pitch in and stage a clean-up time. Maybe it will take half a day once every few months or maybe you can tackle the classroom in 10 minutes or so at the end of every week. This is a good deed that will make the teacher want to give **YOU** an apple (and the janitor will be very happy, too.) You could split the class by task, or divide the room in half and challenge each other to a cleaning-up race.

Desks: Once a week, straighten out the inside of your own desk. You should only keep things in there that you use every day. (Are you really that attached to your paper-clip collection?) It's a good idea to keep a stash of grocery bags in the classroom so you can take some things home if you need to. Baby wipes are great for cleaning pen marks and sticky stains from the tops of desks. Inexpensive brands are fine.

Computers: Turn the computer off, then use a screen wipe to remove dust and dirt

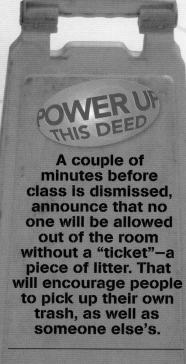

POWER UP THIS DEED

A couple of minutes before class is dismissed, announce that no one will be allowed out of the room without a "ticket"—a piece of litter. That will encourage people to pick up their own trash, as well as someone else's.

from the screen and a soft cloth or paper towel moistened with a tiny drop of water to clean up the keyboard. If the keyboard is really grubby, you might need to mix a little mild dishwashing soap in with the water, but don't go overboard.

Books and magazines: Round 'em up and put them back in their designated spaces. Everyone needs access to reference books, so they need to be kept in a central location.

Walls: There is usually lots of stuff up on display on the school walls and bulletin boards, but it needs to be updated now and again. You can probably live without the March lunch menu by the time April rolls around.

Paper: There is always plenty of paper in the classroom. While it's a great idea to cut down on the amount you use in the first place (for example, by printing on both sides), you can collect old homework in a box to use as scrap paper for working out math problems, etc.

Whiteboards/chalkboards: Give these a good washing down about once a week. Again, baby wipes do a good job on cleaning whiteboards.

READ A STORY TO A LITTLE KID

Do you remember how much you enjoyed storytime when you were a kid? When each story ended, you probably begged for another— and it wasn't just because you wanted to stay up for an extra hour, now was it? Whatever your motive, you can share the imagination-building, stress-busting, brain-boosting experience of reading a story with a little kid in your life. Pick one of your old favorites, or let them choose one of theirs. You could even make up your own story, if you like. Throw in some silly voices—have fun with it. You can bet the little kid will have a great time. Because it's a fact: books are awesome—especially this one, right?

Hi, neighbor!

TURN SOMEONE'S FROWN UPSIDE DOWN

If you see a friend frown as you walk around town,

Think like a clown!

Turn that frown upside down.

WELCOME A NEW KID ON THE BLOCK

The moving van has driven away, the stacks of cardboard boxes are getting shorter, and it appears that your new neighbors are settling in. You couldn't help but notice (because you did ride your bike up and down the street a couple of times) that one of these neighbors appears to be a kid about your age. You know what to do: become a one-kid welcoming committee. Pick your moment carefully. Moving is pretty stressful, and the new kid is probably thinking about the old friends he or she left behind. You can start with a smile, or a wave. If that seems to be OK, then get off your bike and say hi. It could be the start of a beautiful friendship…it could be the end of another good deed…it could be both of these things.

COLLECT WINTER COATS FOR CHARITY

Can you imagine being outside without a winter coat to wear when the temperature really plummets? Do a good deed for less fortunate people in your town, and hold a winter coat drive. Donate the coats to a charity that helps the homeless. This good deed is an example of a warm thought that might actually keep someone warm.

RETURN A SHOPPING CART (BECAUSE THERE'S NO PLACE LIKE HOME)

We've all seen one, abandoned, forlorn, and a long way from home: a lost supermarket shopping cart. How did it get there? Did someone walk to the store, and leave with too much to carry? Was it a dare? Or was the shopping cart suddenly taken with the desire to see the world? However it got there, it shouldn't be there. An estimated two million shopping carts go missing every year, and the impact on the environment is huge. Do the Earth a favor, and if you see a grocery-store cart rolling down the road, drowning in a ditch, or wobbling by the wayside, take it back to its rightful place in the store parking lot.

REST AREA ↗

GIVE A DOG A BOWL OF WATER ON A HOT DAY

When the sun beats down, treat a dog to a delicious bowl of clear, fresh water. You could even throw in a couple of ice cubes for an extra-frosty doggy treat. That four-legged friend will lap it up with gratitude.

TELL GRANDMA AND GRANDPA HOW MUCH THEY MEAN TO YOU

You might call them Bubbe, Nana, Grandma, Granny, Gran, Grammy, Papa, Grandpa, Granda, Granddad, or Gramps. In Spanish, you might call them Abuelita and Abuelito. In Italy, you might say Nonna and Nonno. In Russian, you say Babushka and Dedushka. In German, you might use Oma and Opa.

WHATEVER you call them, pick up the phone and call them. Tell your grandparents how much they really mean to you. You could e-mail them or text them instead, but it will be much nicer for them to hear your voice.

PLANT A TREE

Are you a tree hugger? It's easy to love trees. You can climb up them, sit in their shade on a hot summer's day, hide behind them, hang a tire from their strong branches to make a swing, collect their beautiful fall leaves, and even pluck a ripe red apple from a fruit tree. What's not to like?

So if you're rooting around for a good deed, why not plant a tree? The first step is to choose a site and get permission. If you want to plant a tree in a park or at school or a place of worship, for example, you'll definitely need to find the person in charge and get permission. If you're planning to put down roots at home, your parents will need to give you the go-ahead.

Then, you'll need a tree. Some communities, states, or organizations give away trees for planting programs. Do some research on the Internet to find out if a service like this one is available in your area. You can also buy a tree at the local nursery or garden center. They should be able to give you advice about which type of tree to choose.

Now, get digging! With a shovel, dig a hole as deep as the root-ball and twice as wide. If the soil is really hard, break it up a little with the tip of the shovel. Then remove the container and study the roots. They need to be fairly straight. If they've coiled around and around as they grew in the container, gently straighten them out a little.

Put the tree in the hole, and start filling in the hole with soil. Pack it in with your hands and feet to ensure there are no air pockets. You can mound the dirt up a little around the base of the tree to help hold in water.

Now give the tree a very large drink of delicious water. It might be too little to hug, but if you look after your tree, maybe it will grow up and make you proud.

If you really want to branch out, organize a tree-planting event for your class or club.

POWER UP THIS DEED

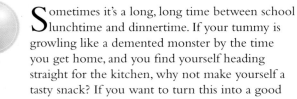

make your sister

an after-school snack

Sometimes it's a long, long time between school lunchtime and dinnertime. If your tummy is growling like a demented monster by the time you get home, and you find yourself heading straight for the kitchen, why not make yourself a tasty snack? If you want to turn this into a good deed, then all you have to do is make your sister (or brother) a snack, too. The monster in your stomach will stop growling, your sister will stop thinking you are a monster in general, and you'll be all set until dinnertime. These snacks are fine to make without an adult's help if you are eight years old and up, but you might want to check that it's all right with your parents before you begin.

P.S. Put away everything in the kitchen when you have finished, and that's another good deed done.

SUPER SILLY SUSHI

You will need:

A tortilla wrap, soft cream cheese, a slice of deli meat, a knife and cutting board, chopsticks

Lay the wrap down on the cutting board and spread it with a thin layer of cream cheese. Add a slice of deli meat on top. Starting at one end, roll the wrap up tightly into a cylinder. Carefully cut through the tube to make five or six slices of "sushi" and serve to your sister (or brother) with chopsticks.

CRACKER STACKERS

You will need:

Whole wheat crackers, deli meat slices, cheese slices, a knife and cutting board

Cut the deli meat and cheese into squares about the same size as the crackers, then use them to fill up cracker sandwiches. Think up as many combos as you can.

PBT

You will need:

Bread for toasting, peanut butter, butter knife. Optional: honey, banana slices

Toast the bread in the toaster and then smooth on some peanut butter while it is still warm. The peanut butter will go all oozy and yum-tastic. You can top with some honey or sliced bananas if you like.

YUMMY YOGURT PARFAIT

You will need:

Plain or vanilla yogurt, fresh fruit (strawberries, bananas, or blueberries), a little honey, granola cereal, a small bowl, a spoon

Fill a small bowl halfway with yogurt and top with some fruit. Drizzle on a little bit of honey (if you like it) and stir this together. Sprinkle granola on top to finish off your treat.

ANIMAL CRACKER SANDWICHES

You will need:

Animal crackers, peanut butter, cream cheese, or jelly, a butter knife

Find a pair of matching animal crackers and make a little sandwich with peanut butter, cream cheese, or jelly. You can use teddy bear-shaped graham crackers, too. Little sisters will love you.

FREAKY FAKE HOT DOGS

You will need:

A hot-dog bun or a slice of bread, a banana, peanut butter, a butter knife

Spread a little peanut butter on the hot dog bun, peel the banana, and lay it inside the bun to look like a hot dog. Strange, huh? But tasty…

this way to a super clean room

THIS WAY TO A SUPER CLEAN ROOM

IN HERE!

CLEAN UP YOUR ROOM (WITHOUT PARENTAL NAGGING)

Sometimes a good deed can be a thing you really like doing. Maybe cleaning your room doesn't exactly fall into that category for you. But this is a good deed that works two ways. Your parents will be incredibly pleased that you took responsibility for tidying up your mess. And you've got to admit it, it is good to climb into a made bed at night. So get to it, and get it over with.

Open your curtains or raise the shade so you can see what level of toxic contamination you are dealing with. You might want to crack a window, too, to air your room out. Pick up and put away the big stuff first. Your room is going to seem cleaner right away with the major clutter under control. Sort out your clothes—yes, even your socks. Put the laundry in the hamper (or wherever you put laundry in your place) and fold up or hang up any clean stuff. Collect all the trash that you find (dare you to look under the bed) and throw it out. If there are any cups or plates, put them in the kitchen. Put books back on the shelves and stack up your DVDs or games in a neat pile. Tidy up any other odds and ends. Make your bed; you just know this is the first thing your mom is going to look at. Run the vacuum cleaner to pick up all the little bits you can't see. And there you go. Another deed done.

P.S. This deed is especially impressive if your parental units haven't been nagging you for days to clean your room. A random act of tidiness will amaze them.

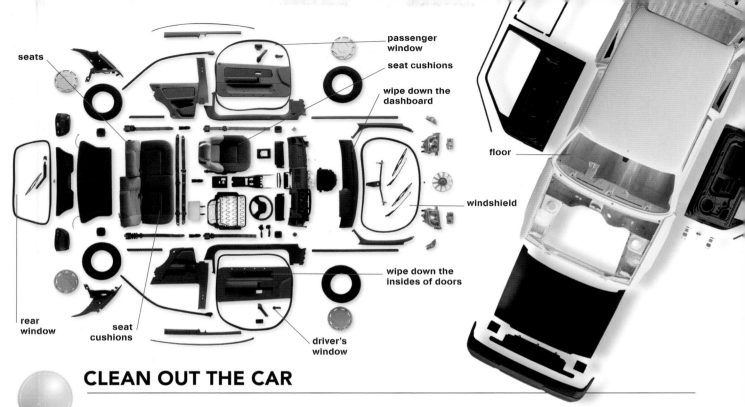

seats

passenger window

seat cushions

wipe down the dashboard

floor

windshield

wipe down the insides of doors

rear window

seat cushions

driver's window

CLEAN OUT THE CAR

Sometimes it feels like your family practically lives in the car or truck, with all the trips to school, to the mall, to practice, to after-school activities, and the grocery store. But your car doesn't have to look quite so lived-in. Why not surprise your family by cleaning out the insides of the car? A bonus for you: you might find a couple of bucks down the backs of the seat cushions. Consider that a tip for a deed well done.

You'll need the vacuum cleaner or a mini-vac, a trash bag (maybe two), window cleaner, and rags or paper towels. Take the floor mats out and shake them down to get rid of

any junk sticking to them. Check beneath and between the seats for trash or debris, and toss it in a bag (unless it's money of course). (Did you find anything surprising? Was it a new form of life?) Then, use the hose attachment of the vacuum cleaner to sweep all the seat cushions. Next, with the floor mats already out of the car you can sweep up the floor area. When the floor is nice and clean, vacuum the floor mats and put them back in. Make the windows sparkle with window cleaner and an old rag or paper towels. Dampen another cloth with water, and use it to wipe down the insides of the doors, the dashboard, and other vinyl surfaces. There you go!

"It takes man deeds to bui reputation, a one bad one

y good
ld a good
nd only
to lose it."

Benjamin Franklin

GIVE YOUR SISTER'S BIKE A TUNE-UP

seat post

top tube

handlebar stem

seat tube

brakes

seat stays

down tube

front derailleur

forks

chain stays

rear derailleur

1

2

3

4

5

Bikes—you can't beat 'em. They get you where you need to be under your own steam; they give you freedom; and they're tons of fun, too.

All you need to do is give your trusty wheels a little TLC from time to time, and you're always good to go. And if you want to turn this into a good deed (and of course you do), why not offer to give your sister's or brother's bike a tune-up at the same time? You should give your bike a thorough check at least once a year, more often if you are a dedicated rider. It's not too tricky…all you need to do is give things a little jiggle and twist to make sure nothing is hanging loose or making a weird noise. Use the steps below as a guide. When you are finished, present your sister or brother with a bill…actually, don't. That is not a good deed. Instead, give his or her bike a clean bill of health.

BASIC TOOLS:

multi-tools: wrenches etc.

cable cutters

puncture repair kit

allen wrenches

air pump

bike stand

POWER UP THIS DEED

WHAT TO DO:

1. Front wheel and brakes: take a look at the brake pads. Are they wearing evenly? Are they so worn out, they need replacing? Squeeze the brakes. Do the pads strike the rim at the same time? Give the front wheel a spin. Does it wobble or go around straight? Wobbly wheels need adjusting.
2. Headset and stem: check the headset adjustment. Squeeze both brakes and, with both wheels on the ground, push the bike backward and forward to see if there is any rattling or movement. There shouldn't be either.
3. Frame: take some time to inspect the frame. Look out for obvious cracks as well as smaller areas of wear and tear that could lead to breakdowns. Check all the nuts and bolts and make sure nothing is loose.
4. Gears: shift through the gears to test for smooth movement. Add lubrication to the chain. Don't use a lot—a couple of drops will be fine.
5. Tire pressure and tread: find out the correct pressure for your bike. Use a pressure gauge to read what the pressure is. If the tires need air, pump some more in. Also, look at the tires to make sure the tread is not bald.

WHILE YOU'RE AT IT, WHY NOT GIVE YOUR BROTHER'S OR SISTER'S BIKE A GOOD CLEAN AT THE SAME TIME? KEEPING THE BIKE SPICK AND SPAN WILL EXTEND THE LIFE OF ALL THE PARTS.

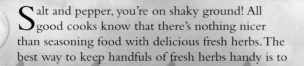

S alt and pepper, you're on shaky ground! All good cooks know that there's nothing nicer than seasoning food with delicious fresh herbs. The best way to keep handfuls of fresh herbs handy is to grow them in a fragrant window box. Basil, parsley, chives, oregano, and thyme are good, easy-growing choices. Plant a mini herb garden for your parents or to give as a gift to your favorite cook.

Create a window box of

WHAT YOU NEED:

You'll need a window box or pot the right size for the spot where you want to keep it, plus herb plants from the garden store (ask for advice about which ones to plant together), potting soil, and some broken-up clay flowerpots. Cover the drainage holes in the window box with broken bits of flowerpot so the soil doesn't drain away with the water. Carefully remove the plants from their pots, keeping the soil intact around their roots. Then fill the box with more soil. Water according to care directions provided with the plants, and introduce your parents to their new friend, Herb.

herbs

WRITE A
THANK-YOU
NOTE

Are you gifted? Do people say you've got real presents…er, make that *presence*? If someone has given you a great gift, a perfect present, or even if they've done something especially nice for you, then as soon as you recycle the wrapping paper (you are going to do that, right?), sit right down and write a thank-you note. Even if you've already said thank you in person, sending your thanks in a letter is an incredibly polite thing to do. It takes only a few minutes, but this is a good deed that will make the gift-giver and the gift-getter feel positively positive about the whole experience.

WHAT YOU NEED:

A blank card or paper

An envelope

A stamp

Crafty stuff like markers, glitter glue, or stickers (optional)

Gratitude—not attitude

WHAT TO DO:

You should send your thank-you note within a few days after you receive something. (It will be like a little gift for the person who sent a gift to you!) Don't write in stiff, fussy language that sounds like robot talk. Instead, just imagine you are talking to the person who gave you the gift, and use your own words. The perfect thank-you note should include a big thank you (duh), mention one thing you particularly like about the present (even if it is a sweater with three arms and no neck opening…come to think of it, that is something to like, right?), and let the gift-giver know what you plan to do with the present, especially if it's money. (If you plan to unravel the sweater and make a huge cat's toy out of the resulting ball of yarn, it is best to keep that under your hat.) The last part is the easiest part: mail it! Don't forget the stamp.

Shukran

Dank je

Hvala

Danke

33

KNIT A HAT OR SCARF FOR A HOMELESS PERSON

Do you think balls of yarn are strictly for the knitting fanatic? Is the closest you've ever come to knitting needles using chopsticks at your favorite Chinese restaurant? Hmmm…well, do you ever knit your brow in concentration? You do? So do you wanna try knitting for real (for a really good cause)? Why not challenge yourself (or your class) to learn how to knit, by knitting a hat or a scarf for someone at a homeless shelter? It's easy once you get the hang of it, it's creative, and it's fun. Lots of people knit to relax, too. (BTW, you know how your mom always tells you to put a hat on when you go outside on a freezing cold day, because you lose most of your body's heat through your head? It's not completely true. The amount of heat released by any part of the body depends on its surface area, so you would lose much more heat on a cold day if you were wearing, say, shorts. Your face, head, and upper chest are more sensitive to temperature change, so covering them up does help you to feel warmer. Who knew?) So make someone a winter warmer-upper. Get a basic knitting book from the library or download step-by-step instructions from the Internet. Grab some needles and yarn and get started. Don't come unraveled if it doesn't work out at first. Try again. Go on, be a knit wit!

INVITE YOUR PARENTS TO A MOVIE NIGHT

Bet your mom and dad would like to get away to the movies, but sometimes that's not as easy as it sounds. In many families, everyone needs to be in at least two places at once. So here's a good deed that will earn you a five-star review from your parents: invite them to a movie night. Make movie tickets to invite them. Rent a DVD that you know they've been wanting to see. Straighten up the room you watch movies in, and throw a couple of extra cushions on the couch. Dim the lights and show mom and dad to their seats. (If you really want to get into it, use a flashlight when you lead them into the living room.) Pop up a big bowlful of popcorn, and leave them in peace to enjoy their home theater. Even critics like your big sister will applaud you.

TAKE A PICTURE OF SOMEONE'S PET AND FRAME IT

Do you know someone who's crazy for cats? Is there a fish fanatic in your life? Do you have a friend or relative who thinks gekkos are the greatest, snakes are superb, or dogs are delightful? People really love their pets. In fact, a recent survey says that 68 percent of American households include some kind of pet. So, if you want to do something really nice for a pet owner, surprise them with a portrait of their beloved animal companion. Take a nice picture that you know will make them smile. (Don't tell the animal to say cheese, though. Except for talking parrots, this will not work.)

You could even make a frame for your photo, or buy an inexpensive one and decorate it with the pet's name, a few hearts, some pawprints, whatever. It's a thoughtful gift that your pet-lover friend or relative will really appreciate, and a very nice deed to do.

P.S. If your friend's pet is a crocodile, you may skip this deed.

GET UP REALLY EARLY AND SET THE BREAKFAST TABLE

Would you call yourself a good morning person? Why not amaze your entire family by getting up super-early (well, at least 10 or 15 minutes before everyone else) and setting the table for breakfast? Clear off the kitchen table. Put out some napkins and cutlery, bowls for cereal, and glasses for juice or milk. If your family are into cereal, set out a few boxes so everyone can choose their favorites. Bring in the morning paper and put it nearby. Breakfast is served, and your deed is complete. Here's a toast to you.

SAVE ENERGY AT HOME

Do a good deed for the planet and help to use energy wisely at home. There's never enough energy to waste, so put some of your own energy into thinking up ways to use less. Here are a few tips:

Turn off the lights when you leave a room. If you're going to be out for more than five minutes, hit the switch.

Turn off your computer, TV, DVD player, and MP3 player when you're not using them. Please.

Don't leave the fridge door open while you stare into the cold depths trying to figure out what snack to eat. Just grab what you need and go.

TRY TO COMPLIMENT EVERYONE YOU MEET TODAY

Hey! You look especially nice today. That color really brings out your eyes. I heard you aced that really tough history test. Nice work! It's fun to be your science partner. You've taught me a lot already. This lunch looks tasty, but then you are a really good cook. Whoa! Nice parallel parking—and on the first try! That was an awesome ollie, dude. You've got a great sense of humor. You always make me laugh. I enjoyed math class today. No, really!

(Psssst, kid. Down here. Do you get the idea? Try to pay a compliment to everyone you meet today. Really try. And no crossing your fingers behind your back when making compliments. Be sincere. Count up how many smiles and thank-yous you get in return. And, by the way, you do look especially nice today.)

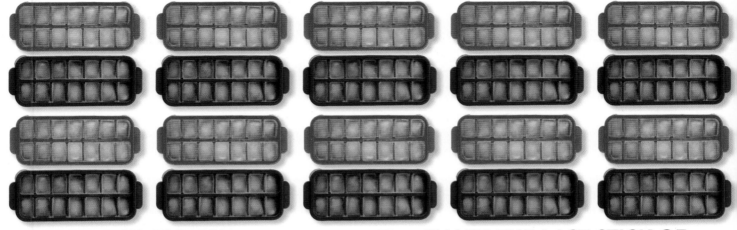

FILL UP THE ICE CUBE TRAY

If you empty the ice cube tray, don't just return it to the depths of the freezer. That is so not cool. Fill it up with water and make new ice cubes. Otherwise, you will get an extremely frosty look from the next person who opens the freezer looking for ice.

KEEP SOMEONE'S SECRET

If someone trusts you enough to tell you a secret, you've just got to keep it, because that's the kind of friend you are. You must fight down the urge to immediately text it to everyone else. Resist the impulse to run down the street screaming out the secret at the top of your lungs. Just say no to the idea of hiring a billboard in the middle of town and printing the secret in huge red letters. Someone trusts you (that's no secret), so make sure you are worth it.

SHARE THE LAST STICK OF GUM IN THE PACK

Down to your very last stick of gum? Tear it in half and share it with your friend. That way, two can chew.

OFFER TO HELP A BLIND PERSON

This is one of the most helpful deeds you can do. People who are blind often use a thin white stick to guide them, or have a guide dog. Usually, they won't need assistance but if you see someone who appears to be blind in difficulty, offer to help them. If they accept, touch your hand to the back of their hand as a signal for them to take your arm. Describe your surroundings to let them know when you are coming to a curb and whether you will be stepping up or down. You're lucky to have sight so, you see, this is a very good deed indeed.

TAKE A TEDDY BEAR TO A CHILDREN'S HOSPITAL

You probably aren't willing to admit it, but chances are there is a teddy bear (or other stuffed animal) in your past. Your little friend (what did you name him?) probably got lots of cuddles and always made you feel better, just by being there. Well, if you cannot bear the thought of a child being lonely in the hospital, why not drop off a new bear at a children's hospital?

It might make someone's stay a little bit more bearable, right?

You and your friends could hold a toy drive for the children's hospital. Contact the volunteer desk for information and ideas. Tell 'em Teddy sent you!

SUPPORT YOUR SISTER'S SOCCER TEAM

Your sister is a soccer superstar. At least, she should feel that way when she is on the field. We all get busy after school and on weekends with our own stuff, but if you want to do a good deed for your sister, go along to her next soccer game, and cheer your head off. You don't need pompoms (phew for that), just plenty of team spirit. She might pretend to ignore you, as sisters do, but she will be thrilled to see you in the stands giving her 100 percent. Go, team!

TEACH A KID HOW TO SHOOT HOOPS

When you were smaller, the basketball net must have seemed a million miles high. Lots of your shots probably fell woefully short of the net. You may have watched the bigger kids sinking shot after shot, wondering if you would ever get to be that good. Well, here's a good deed for a small person: shoot a few hoops with a neighborhood kid, encourage him or her, and show 'em that they have what it takes to (eventually) swish the ball through the net.

Here are some shooting tips to pass along. Get balanced, with your feet shoulder width apart. Keep your eyes on the front of the rim—that's your target. Hold your elbow at an angle and slightly off to the side, so you can see both the basket and the ball. When you shoot, follow through with your hand. Feel like you're putting your hand in the basket.

If you have any other tips, pass them along. Tell the kid he or she is doing great. Someday in the future, when this kid gets to your size, he or she might stop and shoot a few hoops with another kid who's struggling. So, your good deed could go on and on and on. That's more rewarding than even a slam dunk.

BECOME A ONE-KID BOOKMOBILE

Do you have a family friend who loves nothing more than reading, but can't make it to the library due to illness or another reason? Do a great deed for the bookworm in your life by offering to return his or her old library books, and check out some new ones. You'll be like a superhero with a library card instead of a cape! Just ask them to choose a few favorite titles. If nothing is in stock, whisper a very quiet question to the librarian: "EXCUSE ME. My friend loves reading but can't make it to the library. These are some of her very favorite books and authors, but they are not in stock. May I reserve them, please,

and can you help me choose another?" You will earn lots of good deed points (like brownie points but better) not only for helping your friend, but also for having the good manners to whisper in the library. Say it proud, say it not loud: I did a good deed today!

P.S. While you are in the library why not check out a book yourself? Books are cool.

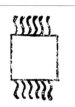

ADDRESS

CHOCOLATE

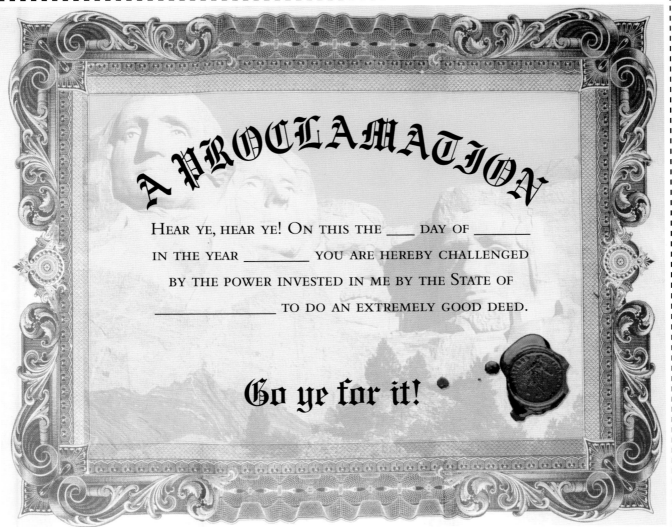

A PROCLAMATION

Hear ye, hear ye! On this the ____ day of _____ in the year _____ you are hereby challenged by the power invested in me by the State of _____ to do an extremely good deed.

Go ye for it!

DK GAMES

Ages 8 years & up

2–4 players

BRING BOARD GAMES TO A NURSING HOME

GOOD DEED, GOOD FUN!

This may not even seem possible, but there was, once upon a time, in a land not very far, far away, an age without computer games. Really! No consoles, no handhelds, no anything. Gasp! OK, we are rubbing it in a little bit here. No matter how awesome the latest game may be, it's also pretty fun breaking out a board game, from the classics you remember, to the old classics your parents enjoyed. It's always good when you can turn something that's good fun into a good deed, so why not take a few games and a bunch of friends to the local nursing home, and hold a games night? No matter who crosses the finish line first, everyone will be a winner.

GIVE AN APPLE TO YOUR TEACHER

Any kid who's ever hoped to be the apple of his teacher's eye has learned that giving an apple to the teacher may help you worm your way into her good books. But why stop there?

Give a banana to the bus driver Give a papaya to the postal worker Give a cantaloupe to the cashier Give a lemon to a librarian Give some strawberries to the school crossing guard Give a coconut to a construction worker Give some raspberries to a receptionist Give a starfruit to a sales clerk Give a peach to a police officer Give a plum to a plumber Give a pear to a pharmacist Give an orange to an office worker Give a fig to a firefighter Give some berries to your babysitter.

DO YOUR CHORES (AND YOUR SISTER'S CHORES)!

You know how parents are. They expect you to do stuff in order to get your allowance. What are they thinking? There are child labor laws, aren't there? I'll bet they tell you stuff like how having responsibilities like weekly chores is an important step in growing up. Heard that one lately? Did they throw in the one about money not growing on trees, too? Yep. Been there, seen it, done it. So do your chores already. You are probably thinking, what kind of good deed is it, if I have to do it anyway? Here's the twist: do your chores (without grumbling) and then, **THEN**, do your sister's chores, too! How good does it get?

TREAT SOMEONE TO ICE CREAM

Did you know that more than a billion gallons of ice cream are sold each year in the United States alone? (How many gallons did you eat?) And that almost 9 percent of all the milk produced by American cows goes to manufacture ice cream? (That's pretty a-moozing, isn't it?) And out of all the kazillions of flavors out there, the most popular one is still good old vanilla? Well, now you know.

For this deed, treat someone special to a very special treat: a delicious ice cream. Cone or cup, sundae or split, just say the magic words, "It's my treat."

MAKE THE BEST GET-WELL CARD EVER

Do you know someone who is under the weather? By that, we don't mean standing out in the rain, although that could be one way to catch something that will put you under the weather. If you've got a friend who's feeling down, a great way to cheer them up is a homemade get-well card. It doesn't matter if you're not exactly Picasso, really throw your creativity behind it (and a little glitter glue helps, too). So, get all your arty, crafty stuff together, and go to town. Your card will be totally unique, just like your friend.

BAKE COOKIES FOR THE FIRE DEPARTMENT (WITHOUT SETTING THE HOUSE ON FIRE IN THE PROCESS)

Firefighters are awesome. They run into burning buildings when everyone else is running out. They don't need a book about good deeds, because they do them every day. The members of your local fire department are responsible not only for firefighting and fire prevention, but also emergency medical services, rescue, disaster response, public education, and community service. Now that's a lot. Why not say thank you with a plate or two of yummy homemade cookies?

BE KIND TO SOMEONE WHO IS NOT SO EASY TO BE KIND TO

Being kind isn't always easy, is it? Especially being kind to someone who isn't that kind, or who treats us badly. Of course, it's good to be kind to everyone, but why not make a special effort to be kind to someone who's not very easy to be kind to? You will feel more than kind of better for it, honest.

HOLD A BIKE RALLY TO TEACH KIDS ABOUT BIKE SAFETY

Following basic safety rules on your bicycle is just as important as making the pedals go around. Why not hold an awesome bicycle safety day to remind riders of all ages about the rules of safe cycling? It's a great deed to do for the community.

Get together with some friends and plan what you'd like to do. A typical bike safety day might include a bike check-up zone, safety helmet fitting tips, a rodeo course, traffic signs quiz, and informational talks. You will need to get permission from your school or community center to hold a safety day. Ask the local police or fire department if they can provide a speaker or an activity for the day. Typical activities offered by the police might include free bicycle registration or road safety talks. The owner of the local bike store might volunteer to run the check-up zone.

There's lots to plan, but the wheels will eventually start to turn. So get on your bike!

MAKE A GET-WELL-SOON KIT FOR SOMEONE WHO IS SICK

It's no fun being sick. You can feel truly awful, and even if you don't exactly feel awful about missing school at first, it can get boring. So, if you know someone who's under the weather, bring him or her some sunshine in the form of a get-well-soon kit. Think about all the stuff that will make your friend a little less bored and collect several items in a box or basket: the loan of a favorite movie or game, some graphic novels or new comic books, the latest issue of a magazine, even a silly joke book. Make a get-well card if you're feeling creative. Check in via e-mail or text just to say hello, and use your phone to film some get-well messages from other friends. The best thing that can happen is that your good deed helps your friend to feel a lot better. What's the worst thing that can happen? You catch what he or she's got!

STICK UP FOR SOMEONE WHO IS BEING MADE FUN OF

While it's good to stand up for yourself, we all need a little help sometimes. If you see someone who needs your help and support (for example, someone who is being bullied), don't just stand there. Stand up for him or her. You'll stand out from the crowd with your outstanding good deed.

KEEP A SMILE ON YOUR FACE FOR THREE STRAIGHT MINUTES

Smiling feels good. If you're feeling down, putting a smile on your face can help change your mood. Smiling also feels good because when we smile, we release endorphins, natural painkillers, and serotonin—stuff that actually does make us feel good, according to doctor types. Smiling helps us stay positive. It's hard to stress out with a smile on your face. Smiling also draws people in. So, for this good deed, keep a smile on your face (that's the easy part) for three whole minutes (that's the somewhat harder part). Feel free to beam or grin, but please, no smirking. Chances are, you will feel better, and the people who see your beautiful smile will feel good, too. And who knows—you might even get a few smiles in return.

A smile is something you can't give away; it always comes back to you.

EVERYONE SMILES IN THE SAME LANGUAGE.

wear a smile...one size fits all.

The shortest distance between two people is a smile.

COLLECT PENNIES AND DONATE THEM TO CHARITY

See a penny?

Pick it up.

The rest of the day, you'll have good luck.

See a whole bunch of pennies sitting around collecting dust in a jar?

Do you dare to stick your hand down the back of the sofa where the lost pennies live?

Collect all the pennies and loose change in the house and donate it to your favorite charity.

START A GOOD DEED WEEK AT YOUR SCHOOL

Imagine if everyone in your school participated in a Good Deed Week. Together, you'd generate so much good feeling that even a surprise pop quiz in algebra would feel practically like a party. (OK, maybe not. This might be going too far.) Talk with your teacher or principal about organizing this. There are loads of fantastic ideas for activities and events online. Or, you can get a team together and brainstorm your own ideas. Get inspired, and get ready to spread a little happiness throughout the hallways, a little love around the lockers, and grins in the gym.

P.S. If you like algebra, that's great. Sorry for making an algebra joke. I'll bet you did really well on the pop quiz.

SWEEP THE SIDEWALK

Q. Why was the broom late?

A. It overswept.

Get out there and give the sidewalk in front of your house or apartment building a clean sweep! Best to wear rubber gloves for this deed. Grab a broom, a dustpan, and a trash bag. Pick up any garbage you encounter and bag it. Even old chewing gum…eeeeeew. Sweep the dust and small debris into a pile then use the broom to push it into the dustpan. Tip everything into the trash bag, then throw it in the garbage. Remember, step on a crack, and you'll break someone's back…so be careful out there.

VOLUNTEER AT THE LOCAL ANIMAL SHELTER

Want a really warm fuzzy feeling inside? Why not volunteer to help out at your local animal shelter? Look in the phone book or online to find your nearest shelter, and give them a call to ask how you could help. Whether you are cleaning cages or walking dogs, you'll make your four-legged (and two-legged) friends very happy.

Squeak! Squeak!

TRANSLATION: Is that a cat over there?

TREAT SOMEONE TO BREAKFAST IN BED

MAKE SOMEONE'S MORNING

Make someone's morning by preparing and serving them an extra-special breakfast in bed. If you can't cook, don't worry. A simple bowl of cereal will taste a lot nicer when it's been served with a smile. If you do know your way around the kitchen, why not whip up one of these tasty treats? Whether it's Mother's Day, Father's Day, or any old day, treating someone to breakfast in bed will show them how much you appreciate him or her. It's the ultimate happy meal (and a very tasty good deed indeed).

WHAT TO DO:

Think about your menu and make sure you have all the stuff you need. Set your alarm clock and get up nice and early. Tiptoe around the kitchen so you don't wake anyone up. Prepare a tray to serve breakfast on. If you can't find a tray, improvise with a platter or basket. Add cutlery and a pretty napkin, and decorate it with a fresh flower (if you have one handy). If you don't have a flower, you could make a paper one or print a picture of one and cut around it. Virtual flowers make people happy, too. Pour a small glass of juice and put it on the tray. It might be nice to include the morning paper or a new magazine. When the tray is ready, prepare breakfast, then serve. You have officially made someone's day.

P.S. Remember to clean up after yourself in the kitchen. Leaving a mess is a bad deed.

YUMMY CHEESY EGGS ON TOAST

SERVES 1

1 slice of bread, **2** eggs, **2** tbsp. grated cheese (cheddar, jack, or Swiss), **1** tsp. butter

TO MAKE:

Beat the eggs in a small bowl with a whisk or fork until they are combined. Stir in the cheese. Put a small non-stick pan on the stove over low to medium heat, and add the butter. When it foams, tip in the eggs. Use a wooden or plastic spatula to stir the eggs until they are cooked soft or firm, depending on how the recipient likes to eat them. Meanwhile, toast a slice of bread. When the eggs are ready, tip them onto the toast and serve with a smile.

DELUXE AND DELICIOUS EGG SCRAMBLE

SERVES 4

8 eggs, **¼** cup milk, **½** tsp. salt and a dash of pepper, **2** tbsp. butter, **1** chopped tomato, **1** tbsp. sliced green onion tops (be careful with the knife!)

TO MAKE:

In a large mixing bowl, beat the eggs, milk, salt, and pepper together until combined. Melt the butter in a non-stick pan over medium-low heat until it foams a little. Pour in the egg mix and turn down the heat to low. As the egg begins to set on the sides of the pan, use a spatula to lift the edges so the uncooked egg can run underneath. Continue lifting and folding until the eggs are almost completely set. Add the tomato and green onion and fold in. When the eggs are cooked just right, serve while they are still hot.

BRILLIANT BREAKFAST BURRITOS

SERVES 4

1 cup canned refried beans, or cooked black beans mashed slightly with a fork, **4** corn or flour tortillas, **2** tbsp. chopped onion, **½** cup chopped tomatoes, **½** cup salsa (any kind you like), **4** tbsp. low-fat sour cream or plain yogurt, **2** tbsp. chopped cilantro leaf

TO MAKE:

Mix the beans, onions, and tomatoes. Put the tortillas between two sheets of slightly damp paper towels and microwave on high for 15 seconds to warm. Lay the tortillas on a cutting board or work surface. Divide up the bean mix between them, spooning it into the middle of each. Fold the tortillas to enclose the filling. Place all four tortilla rolls on a microwave-safe plate and spoon salsa over each one. Cook on high for 15 seconds to warm through, then carefully put each burrito on a plate and top with sour cream and cilantro. Arriba!

SUPER FLUFFY CINNAMON FRENCH TOAST

SERVES 4

1 egg, **2** egg whites, **¼** cup milk, **¼** tsp. vanilla extract, **¼** tsp. ground cinnamon, **8** slices bread, slightly stale is best

TO MAKE:

Put the egg and egg white into a small shallow bowl and whisk until foamy. Whisk in the milk, vanilla extract, and cinnamon. Dip two slices of bread into the egg mix, and turn to coat both sides. Let the extra drip back into the bowl. Heat up a non-stick frying pan and put in the bread. Cook until one side is nice and toasty brown, and flip. It will take about two minutes to cook each side. Put on a plate, cover with a clean dish towel or paper towel, and repeat with the remaining bread and egg mix. Serve with maple syrup. Yum.

HAVE A CLEAN-UP PARTY IN THE PARK

Like most kids, you probably have lots of happy memories of long afternoons in the park. Did you swing so high you thought you were going to fly off and up into space? Remember when you conquered the monkey bars? And nothing was better than hearing the distant jingle of the ice cream truck. The park's been a special place for you. Now it is your turn to do something special for it. Arrange a clean-up party with your friends, and spruce up the park so that other kids can have happy memories there—just like you.

Once you've found a park that needs a little TLC, make a plan of action. List what needs doing: picking up trash, giving everything a good sweep, planting some flowers, wiping down play areas, or raking up leaves. Then contact the parks department (you'll find them in the phone book or online) and explain what you'd like to do. When you have permission (and ONLY then), pick a day, get a group of kids together, and gather all the stuff you will need: rakes, brooms, trash bags, buckets, rags, bedding plants or seeds, and so on. Then, get to it! It's not a walk in the park, but it's a great good deed.

COLLECT TOYS FOR THE HOMELESS SHELTER

These days a lot of us have too much stuff (have you looked in your room lately?), but many people (including kids) have very little. You can help make a difference for needy kids in your area by collecting donations of new or gently used toys. You don't have to wait for the holiday season. Kids like toys all year round. Phone the local homeless shelter or charitable organization and ask what needs and requirements they have. Then get collecting. Ask an adult to help you deliver the toys. You will definitely make someone, somewhere, smile, which is a good deed in itself.

LEAVE A GET-WELL CARD FOR A STRANGER

Little things mean a lot sometimes. They really do. Next time you are buying someone a birthday card, pick up an extra get-well card (you can make one, too). Write a kind message inside, and drop it off at your local hospital. Ask the nice people at the reception desk to please give the card to someone who will appreciate it,

SHARE A BOOK WITH SOMEONE

Are you one of those kids who always has your nose in a book? Would you even go so far as to describe yourself as a bookworm? If you are, that's great news. Reading rocks. Reading is one of the best ways there is to open your world wide up and stretch your brain. For this good deed, introduce someone else to the joy of reading by picking the perfect book for them and passing it along. Tell them that you chose it especially for them, and why you think they will like it. Get someone reading and this deed is complete.

P.S. Don't give away this book just yet! You still have some deeds to do.

DO YARD CHORES FOR A NEIGHBOR WHO NEEDS HELP

Do you know someone who can't get around as well as they used to? Maybe there is an elderly person who finds the tough yard work jobs just too difficult. Offer to pitch in and help with the yard chores. You could tidy up, cut the grass, weed the garden or flowerbeds, plant seeds or bulbs, or water the lawn. Offer service with a smile, and refuse all payment that isn't a tall glass of lemonade or water poured over an iceberg's worth of cubes.

P.S. If you get together with your friends and attack the lawn, you'll be done in no time at all.

VISIT A FREE-CLICK WEBSITE

Even if your allowance has long since bitten the dust, you can still help your favorite causes and donate money to charity. All you have to do is click a mouse. Visit a "free-click" donation site for a charity you support on the Internet. Click a donation button, and that's that.

NOW ON WITH THE BOOK...

EXTRA! EXTRA!
READ ALL ABOUT IT!
Local youth involved in good deed shocker!

PUT FLOWERS IN YOUR NEIGHBOR'S NEWSPAPER

Sources today report that a kid matching your description got up really early, right after the "thunk" of the morning paper hitting the driveway, tiptoed over to the neighbor's house, opened up the paper, and slipped a fresh flower inside to surprise said neighbor. There were unconfirmed reports that the kid was dressed in pajamas and slippers. When asked for comment, Mr. A. Neighbor replied, "I don't know what to say. I usually expect bad news when I open this thing. The kid's done a good deed."

GIVE YOUR WAITER A FIVE-STAR REVIEW

Don't be a restaurant critic, be a good-deed giver. Leave a secret compliment to your waiter or waitress next time you go out to eat with your family. Write a note telling him or her how much you enjoyed their service and attention, pointing out any nice things they did for you. Leave it (along with a tip!) when you pay the bill.

COLLECT CANNED GOODS FOR A FOOD BANK

Some people have a tough time putting a meal on the table. A recent study says one in nine Americans needs help with food. You can make a difference by collecting canned goods and non-perishable foods for donation to your local food bank. Call them up and ask them for a list of their most-needed items. If you get approval, set up a collection box in the classroom. Maybe you can challenge another classroom to match your donation.

P.S. Many food banks get donations around the holidays, but people are hungry every day, all year.

TAKE A NICE PICTURE OF YOURSELF AND LEAVE IT ON MOM'S PILLOW

OK, so maybe you didn't put your dirty gym clothes in the basket, maybe you left a grubby handprint on the fridge handle when you were in a hurry to get a drink, maybe you didn't say thanks for the ride to soccer practice, and maybe (just maybe) you forgot to do that thing mom was reminding you to do, whatever that was. But chances are, even if you did all these things in the same day, your mom still loves you. Give her a surprise: take a picture of yourself. First, remove any peanut butter, chocolate, or dirt from your face. Say cheese and smile big. Then print the photo out and leave it on her pillow. This deed is almost 100 percent guaranteed to make her happy.

You welcomed a new kid (see p.19), now go that extra mile and welcome a whole family to the neighborhood. Remember how funny it felt when your family moved? New room, new home, new neighborhood, new kids to make friends with, new school, new everything, in fact. Sometimes it must have felt like too much "new" altogether. While moving can be exciting, it's also pretty tough trying to find your feet in a new place. Helping your new neighbors to feel welcome and offering them a little kindness is a fantastic good deed. And who knows? You might just make yourself a new friend, too! Here are a few good ways to be a good neighbor.

WELCOME A NEW FAMILY TO THE NEIGHBORHOOD

WELCOME

1. Say hello! Introduce yourself! Smile! Moving in is kind of stressful, and your new neighbors might not be able to stop and chat, but they will remember you as the friendly kid who said "Hi."

2. Bring over a yummy gift...some homemade cookies, maybe, or a tray of brownies or a half-dozen cupcakes.

3. If your new neighbors have little kids, put together a gift bag of coloring or sticker books, crayons, markers, and juice boxes. Their parents will really appreciate you giving them something new to do while they unpack.

4. Make a list of useful places in the neighborhood (grocery store, playground, library...things like that). Download and print a local map and mark the locations, so everything will be easy to find.

5. Collect takeout menus from local pizza delivery places and restaurants. Deliver them!

6. If you have an extra phone book, pass it along.

7. Pick up bus and subway maps and share them with your new neighbors.

8. If you're going to the grocery store, stop by and ask if there is anything they need. This is something super-busy people really appreciate.

9. Introduce them to some other neighbors. If someone down the street has kids the same age, or has similar interests, hook them up. The more people they meet, the easier it will be to fit in.

10. Keep saying hello. Wave when you ride by on your bike. Greet everyone by name. Do a good deed and be a good neighbor.

ADOPT A CLASSROOM PROJECT FOR THE SCHOOL YEAR

Does your class have class? Show everyone what a class act your class is by adopting a volunteer project for the year. Kids of any age can find an appropriate volunteering opportunity. Sit down with your teacher and brainstorm some ideas. Decide how much time you can give, and what kind of project you would like to do. You might even find a way to connect your project with something you are studying in class. Figure out all the nuts-and-bolts stuff, such as what permissions you need. Giving back to the community through a volunteer project is a deed well done. You deserve an A+.

DO A LOAD OF LAUNDRY

How do all those clean clothes get in your closet or chest of drawers? Is it magic? The last time you saw a pair of socks or a T-shirt, they were lying on the floor in a heap, and then, abracadabra, they're clean again and ready for you to make smelly. It's time to let you in on a little secret. Clothes don't get clean by magic… someone puts them in the washing machine, adds some detergent, presses a few buttons, then waits for a bit until the machine stops making a noise, then hangs them up to dry in the sun or puts them in the dryer, then irons them, folds them up, then puts them away in your room. (Whoa! Actually that is kind of magical.) Perform the amazing, incredible, never-before-seen task of doing a load of laundry to complete this good deed. If you don't know how it all works, find someone to fill you in. It's easy once you know how. Your gym socks will thank you.

WASH INSIDE OUT

FOR FULL INSTRUCTIONS SEE MAGIC WASH

100% GOOD DEED

© UNOFFICIAL OFFICIAL PRODUCTS

CARVE A PUMPKIN FOR SOMEONE AT HALLOWEEN

Nothing says Halloween like a glowing jack-o-lantern in every window. But sometimes, if there isn't a kid in the house, it's tempting to skip the pumpkin carving. When you buy your pumpkin this year, buy an extra one. Use your best skills to carve it into a super-cool jack-o-lantern, and give it to someone. It's not a trick, it's a real treat.

Easy, but be careful with the knife.

FEED YOUR NEIGHBOR'S DOG OR CAT WHILE THEY ARE AWAY (FOR FREE)

Here, kiddy, kiddy! So your neighbor went on vacation, but we weren't invited. I might just scratch the sofa a little more than usual, you know.

Nice to see you. My tail's wagging already. After you feed us and give us some water, wanna play a little?

Sheesh. You dogs are not very particular, are you?

This kid comes all the way over here twice a day to feed us and check we're OK. And he's doing it for free! I say that's worth wagging your tail for.

Whatever. I'll throw in a purr.

ASK AN ELDERLY FRIEND OF THE FAMILY IF YOU CAN HELP THEM WITH SOME CHORES AROUND THE HOUSE

Help is a very nice four-letter word. To do this deed, here's what to do: speak with an elderly family friend and find out if you can offer them help in any way. It's as simple as that, and as nice as that.

DONATE YOUR ALLOWANCE

Is your allowance burning a hole in your pocket? How would you like to use it to buy a shiny new halo? OK, so haloes actually aren't for sale, it's true. But if you donate your allowance to a relief organization or to a charity you support, you just might see a halo appearing.

MAKE A GOOD DEEDS BOX

One way to remind your classmates that kindness makes a difference is by making a good deeds box. Find a large shoebox with a lid, and carefully cut a slot in the lid large enough for notes to be dropped in. You can leave it nice and plain because the good stuff is what goes inside, or you can go to town and decorate the box. Ask your teacher if you can put it in the corner of the classroom. Here's how the box works: ask everyone to do a good deed for someone every couple of weeks, write about it, and put it in the box. The notes should describe the deed, the reaction to it, and how doing the good deed made you feel. Once a month or so, ask your teacher to pull out a few papers at random and read them to the class, keeping the ID of the deed-doer a secret. You'll be surprised at how much happiness fits into a plain old shoebox.

BE A VOLUNTEER AT THE LOCAL LIBRARY

Support your local library, enjoy helping others, and clock up serious good deed points by volunteering at the library. Large libraries usually have loads of programs that you can get involved with, from adult literacy classes, after-school homework clubs, book buddy programs for little kids, and computer skills classes. The only downside is, you'll have to whisper the whole time (just kidding). Make friends with your local librarian and ask how you can get involved. You'll close the chapter on yet another good deed, and everyone will live happily ever after. The end.

Q. What building has the most stories?
A. The library.

Q. Why did the librarian slip and fall on the library floor?
A. She was in the non-friction section.

PUSH YOUR COUSIN ON THE SWING (AND LET YOUR AUNT HAVE A BREAK)

Do you remember how you loved to be pushed on the swing when you were younger? Almost nothing felt as good as whooshing back and forth through the air on a summer day, pumping your legs so you almost felt like you were going to fly off. Give your little cousin that same thrill by offering to push her on the swing at the park. Show her how you can move your arms, legs, and body when you're swinging, so she can learn how to control the swing. It takes concentration, but most elementary-age kids can handle it.

POWER UP THIS DEED

If it's OK with her parents, treat her to a popsicle or ice cream cone from the ice cream truck afterward.

IF SOMEONE DOES A GOOD DEED FOR YOU, PASS IT ON THREE MORE TIMES IN THAT DAY

One good turn deserves another, they say. (Who are these "they" people who go around saying things?) But you—yes, you—want to go beyond what is deserved. You want to do good turns until you're dizzy. Here's an easy way to do it: if someone does a good turn for you, pass it on three more times—in the same day.

MAKE TREAT BAGS FOR KIDS IN THE HOSPITAL

Being in the hospital is especially tough on kids. As you know, kids were made for the great wide-open spaces. So a kind volunteer project for you, your class, or your friends would be to create special treat bags to brighten up a hospitalized kid's day. Call the hospital volunteer people to discuss your plans, and find out if there are rules about what you can and cannot give. Ask people to donate a number of small items that you know kids like: small toys, art supplies like paints, markers, or crayons, sticker books, puzzle books, coloring books, healthy snacks, something to cuddle, and so on. Spend a little time making your treat bag look great. You could wrap all the little things in tissue paper and then put them in a gift bag you've decorated yourself. Include a kid-to-kid get-well soon message. What a treat!

PLANT SOME WILD FLOWERS

Give the whole world a beautiful bouquet by planting some wildflowers. Grab a couple of packs of wildflower seeds at the garden center. The friendly people there can give you advice about which ones to choose for your location. The best time to plant is in the spring. The best spot is anywhere sunny that has good drainage (that means water doesn't collect there after it rains.) Follow the instructions on the packet and before long, things will be coming up roses for you. Well, not really roses. But you knew that.

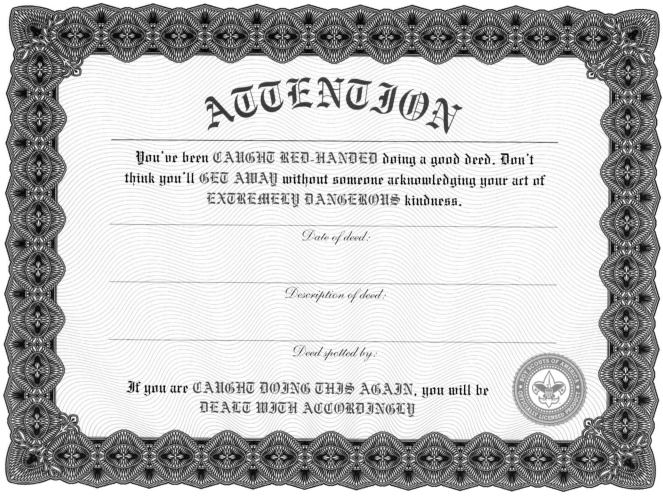

ATTENTION

You've been CAUGHT RED-HANDED doing a good deed. Don't think you'll GET AWAY without someone acknowledging your act of EXTREMELY DANGEROUS kindness.

Date of deed:

Description of deed:

Deed spotted by:

If you are CAUGHT DOING THIS AGAIN, you will be DEALT WITH ACCORDINGLY

BOY SCOUTS OF AMERICA · OFFICIALLY LICENSED PRODUCT

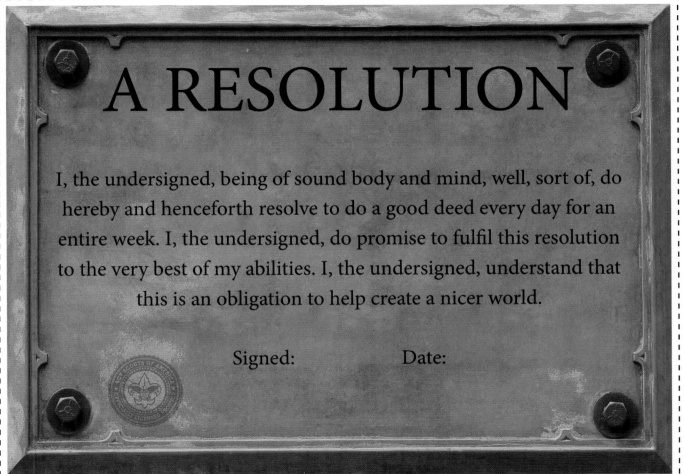

A RESOLUTION

I, the undersigned, being of sound body and mind, well, sort of, do hereby and henceforth resolve to do a good deed every day for an entire week. I, the undersigned, do promise to fulfil this resolution to the very best of my abilities. I, the undersigned, understand that this is an obligation to help create a nicer world.

Signed: Date:

SEND SOMEONE A PACKET OF FLOWER SEEDS

How would you like your good deeds to blossom and bloom? In the early springtime, pick out a packet of flower seeds from the garden center and send it to someone special. Write a note to let them know why you'd like to give them a bouquet of flowers every day. With a little care, a little sunshine, and a little water, the seeds will grow into beautiful, sweet-smelling blooms. You couldn't pick a nicer deed.

MAKE A DECK OF GOOD DEEDS

Hey, poker face! Want to do a good deed, but can't think of anything? You'll never be without inspiration if you make a deck of good deeds. You'll need a few sheets of light cardboard, a pencil and ruler, some scissors, and markers or a pen. Use the pencil and ruler to mark each sheet of cardboard into smaller rectangles, 2½ x 3½ inches. (There are 54 cards in a deck of playing cards, including two jokers, but you can make any number of cards you like.) Write a good deed on one side of each card. Use ones from this book or think up your own. When you have a need for a deed, you can shuffle the cards and pick a deed at random. You could also challenge your friends to pick any card and do that good deed.

ROLL YOUR NEIGHBOR'S TRASH CANS BACK UP THE DRIVEWAY AFTER PICK-UP

Every week, everybody rolls those trash cans down to the street, then after the garbage trucks roll through, they roll 'em right back up. So if you want to do a simple good deed that really rocks, roll your own cans back up the driveway and then bring your neighbor's cans back home as well. Done!

TIP YOUR TAXI DRIVER

Did you ever stop to think what might happen if your mom or dad had a taxi meter in the family car? What if they put the meter on every time they drove you back and forth to school, to the mall, to your friend's house, to practice, or to the game? Imagine what kind of bill you'd have run up already (and you're still a kid). Whoa! I hope you've been paying attention in math class, because that would be a seriously large number, and I don't think your allowance would quite cover it. So how do you tip the sole owner and proprietor of Mom's Taxi Service, the most reliable ride in town?
Give your mom the day off. Plan to walk, get a ride with a friend, or take the bus, if at all possible. Tell your mom that you really appreciate the way she runs the roads for you. Give her a hug and tell her to enjoy some free time.

DARE SOMEONE TO DO A GOOD DEED

LEAVE AN ANONYMOUS NOTE IN A LIBRARY BOOK TO CHEER UP THE NEXT PERSON WHO BORROWS IT

Serendipity /seren'dipiti/
noun
The art of finding something valuable by looking for something else.

Bring a little bit of serendipity to someone's life by leaving a secret note tucked inside a library book when you return it. Think about what might inspire or surprise someone. Maybe you can write something funny, or some simple words of encouragement. You could even try a quote or a poem. Be serendipitous!

P.S. If the book you are returning is a whodunit, please do not use the note to tell the next reader who did it. That's not fair.

BUY A COLD DRINK OR A BOTTLE OF WATER FOR A POLICE OFFICER

Fighting crime on a hot day is bound to make you thirsty. Offer an icy cold can of soda or a super-chilled bottle of water to a police officer when the temperature rises. You can take the opportunity to thank him or her for helping to keep your neighborhood safe. Your good deed will certainly be an arresting one…

GIVE SOMEONE'S DOG A SHAMPOO

Do dogs have bad hair days? Or would they call them bad fur days? Or are they barking about something else altogether? Unlike you, dogs don't need a bath that often, unless they get into something greasy or extra-dirty, or start to smell a little too dog-gy. You can do a good deed for your favorite dog owner by offering to bathe and shampoo his or her four-legged friend. Bathing a dog is a bit tricky. Some dogs get scared, and handling a wet dog who wants to do nothing more than shake off the water all over the place isn't easy. But if you get everything you need ready in advance, wear old clothes, and bring along plenty of towels, before you know it your new friend will be wagging a shiny, clean tail at you.

BE A VOLUNTEER

How can you help people and animals who really need it most? Be a volunteer! Spend some of your free time helping other people. By helping others, you help yourself. Fight for a cause you really believe in. Whether it's looking after people in your community who need a hand, helping to care for animals, or protecting the environment, you can make a difference, even if you are only a kid.

How do you get into volunteering? You can find opportunities through the local Boy Scouts troop, for example, or other clubs and organizations. Churches, synagogues, and mosques also offer volunteer programs. You could also check with your school or city parks department. This book might even inspire an idea or two.

What are you waiting for? Help someone today.

HELP! HELP! Everybody needs it. You've got it. What can you do about it? Volunteer!

HELP SOMEONE WITH HIS OR HER HOMEWORK

⭐⭐⭐

👤

Homework. Home. Work.
You don't exactly want to work when you come home, do you? You want to play. But before you can, you have to make sure your homework is in the bag. If you want to do a good deed, help someone with his or her homework. As you go over your assignment together, you will learn, too. A little encouragement, a few hints, a couple of tips, and both of you will be done with the "work" part of homework in no time at all.

LISTEN TO SOMEONE WHO REALLY NEEDS TO TALK

⭐

👤

Listen up! There are times when we need to be alone. There are times when we need to laugh. There are even times when we need chocolate. But sometimes, what we really need is someone to talk to. If you know someone needs to open up to someone, be a friend, do a good deed, and listen. Really listen. Go somewhere with no distractions and give them your complete attention. Encourage them to be open. Make eye contact and smile. Make them feel important. Let them know that you hear what they are saying.

SAY THANK YOU TO THREE PEOPLE TODAY WHO YOU'VE NEVER THANKED BEFORE

Two little words: thank you. It doesn't take any time at all to say them, but sometimes we are in a hurry and we forget. For this good deed, think of three people who really deserve to hear these words. Maybe it's the bus driver you see every morning, or the school crossing guard, or the nice librarian who reserved the Harry Potter book for you. Smile and say thank you to them. Those two little words said three little times will equal one big good deed.

TRY TO LAST THE ENTIRE DAY THINKING ONLY GOOD THINGS

Think good thoughts. Wonder who came up with that? It probably wasn't a person who left their lunch on the school bus, then was five minutes late for English class, then got picked on by that mean kid in the hallway, then tripped over their shoelaces and looked like a dork in front of everybody. If life leaves you scrambled, stay sunny side up. In fact, why not challenge yourself to last the entire day with only good thoughts in your head? Tell your inner grouch to hit the road for a day.

P.S. It may be best not to attempt this deed on a Monday.

WRITE YOUR GRANDPARENTS A NICE LETTER

Hi!

I know it's been a long time since I've written you a letter. (It's been a really long time since I've written anyone a letter, thanks to e-mail and IM-ing and everything.)

But I think about you and I thought I would write as if we were talking together. I really love all the special times we've had and the fun stuff we do together. I also want to tell you I miss you when we are apart. So that's why I'm writing this letter.

yours truly,

me

GRANDMOM, GRANDAD

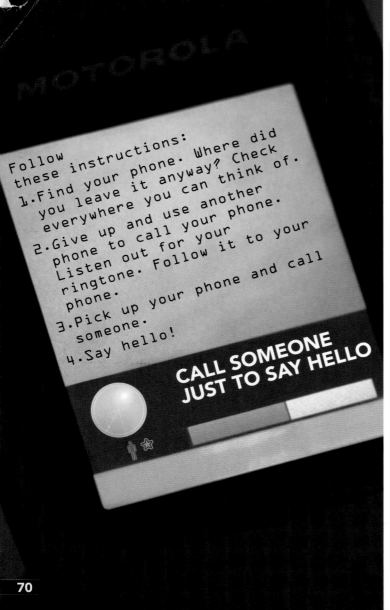

Follow these instructions:
1. Find your phone. Where did you leave it anyway? Check everywhere you can think of.
2. Give up and use another phone to call your phone. Listen out for your ringtone. Follow it to your phone.
3. Pick up your phone and call someone.
4. Say hello!

CALL SOMEONE JUST TO SAY HELLO

CELEBRATE SOMEONE'S ACHIEVEMENT WITH A CUPCAKE

Actions speak louder than words. They really do, unless maybe you are comparing wriggling your ears a tiny bit to screaming at the top of your lungs. But do you know what speaks louder than actions? That's right: cupcakes. If you know someone who has done something great, congratulate her with your words and then take action. Buy her a cupcake, one with sprinkles on the top and everything. Your tasty good deed just may be the icing on the (cup) cake for her wonderful achievement.

GIVE A DVD TO SOMEONE

Did you know that "DVD" originally stood for Digital Video Disk? Some of its creators thought it should instead stand for Digital Versatile Disk, because it could be used in many non-video ways. Its official specifications call it a "DVD" without explaining what the letters mean.

So now you know! But anyway, back to the GD. That's "Good Deed." Here's what to do. Go through your own movie collection (you could tidy everything up and put disks back in their boxes while you are at it) and sort out movies that you no longer want to watch. Think of someone who might enjoy the film, and pass the DVD along to him or her. That's one Darned Valuable Deed done.

SMILE WHEN YOU PICK UP THE PHONE

People say you can hear a smile in someone's voice even if you can't see it. So show your good manners and put on a happy face before you pick up the telephone. The person calling you will notice, unless it is one of those pre-recorded robot-style voice messages.

GIVE YOUR LITTLE SISTER A TEA PARTY

Maybe it doesn't feel like it sometimes, but your little sister (or cousin or niece) probably really looks up to you. And it's not just because she's such a squirt and you're so tall. If you'd like to give her a special treat and do a good deed at the same time, you could throw a tea party for her. Invite some of her real friends or just stick to teddy bears and dolls. If the weather is nice, hold your party outside. A pretty tablecloth and a vase of fresh flowers will set the scene. Put out a couple of plates of cookies and prepare some simple sandwiches. You could cut them into shapes with cookie cutters. Even a trusty PB and J (Peanut Butter and Jelly to the uninitiated) feels special when it's cut in a different shape. Serve lemonade, fruit tea, or decaffeinated tea if you like. Watch your little sister sparkle.

P.S. If your guests are all toys, just set up her tea set, fill up the toy teapot with water, and use play food. She'll still love you for it, especially if you talk to her stuffed animals.

LEAVE A SURPRISE IN YOUR SISTER'S ROOM

I know what you're thinking, but a slimy, yucky frog, a lumpy, bumpy toad, or a leggy, scary spider are three things NOT to leave as a surprise in your sister's room. If you are even tempted to do this, maybe you need to go back to the front of this book and start the good deeds all over again. What you DO need to do, is leave a pretty flower or a helium balloon in your sister's room. Now that's a nice deed.

POWER UP THIS DEED

Attach a note to let her know why you think she is awesomely cool and the sweetest sibling around.

SAY NO TO A PLASTIC BAG TODAY

All those plastic bags you bring home from the store probably end up in a great big ugly landfill. Each year, there are an estimated 500 billion plastic bags handed out, but less than 3 percent of those are recycled. That's bad news, because polyethylene bags can take up to 1,000 long years to biodegrade. If that's not enough to put you off, they give off greenhouse gases while they do it. So, get in the habit of taking a reusable cloth bag to the store. If you are offered a plastic bag, smile, and say no thank you.

CALL UP A FRIEND AND TELL HIM WHY HE'S A FRIEND

Hello? Oh, nothing really. I was just thinking about how you are such a cool friend. I just wanted you to know that. OK. No, that's it, really. See ya.

ENTERTAIN AT A NURSING HOME

Maybe the closest you've ever been to a ham is in a sandwich, but if you've got the acting bug, or sing in the choir, or participate on the speech team or drama club, or do a little stand-up comedy, or if your friends have a band, then why not show off your skills to a very appreciative audience at your local nursing home? Call up and offer to entertain a group of seniors. Their applause will feel pretty good, and so will knowing you've made a bit of a difference to their day.

CLEAN UP A CAMPSITE

The legendary camping motto "Leave no trace" is supposed to encourage people to leave a campsite looking as if no one has ever been there before. But sadly, not everyone is as considerate of the environment as they should be. Get a gang of friends together and volunteer to spend a morning cleaning up your favorite camping spot. First, contact the parks and recreation department and let them know you'd like to do it. Gather together a few basic tools like brooms, rakes, buckets and rags, and a few trash bags. When you get to the camp, do a quick inspection and make a list of what needs doing. Then just do it! Clear trails, rake gravel paths, sweep up, wash down picnic tables, and, most importantly, collect trash, recycle what you can, and dispose of the rest. If there are lots of you, you'll be done in no time. Mother Nature will thank you.

LEND SOMEONE A COAT WHEN IT'S COLD

This is one of those examples of simple, everyday kind things you can do for someone. The days might be long gone when a gentleman covered a mud puddle with his coat so nobody had to step in it. Chances are if you did that, the person would just look at you funny, and you aren't going to make your mom very happy if you come home with a mud-soaked coat, are you? But if someone is shivering and freezing, and practically turning blue with the cold, then offer to lend them your coat, even for a little bit. It's a n-ice deed to do.

MAKE A WORK OF ART AS A SURPRISE FOR SOMEONE

When you were little, your refrigerator was probably covered with all the art masterpieces you created at preschool or kindergarten. Maybe you've moved on from finger painting, but wouldn't it be nice to surprise your parents or grandparents with a drawing, painting, collage, or photograph created just for them? Dig out some art materials and get inspired. You go, Picasso!

hotdog

CREATE A PLAYLIST FOR YOUR MOM AND DAD

You might have noticed that, being a kid, you are pretty good with technology. You also might have spotted that, being parents, your mom and dad might not be so used to the whole wired world. (Not all parents are technophobes…look it up…but lots are. They didn't grow up with all the stuff you did, back in the dark ages.) Anyway, a great deed to do for parents (or sisters or brothers) is to download all their favorite CDs onto a music software program, and create playlists for different times of the day. You could make one for mom's commute, or a playlist of songs everyone likes for family car trips. No more rummaging around for CDs—just push a button and you're ready to rock.

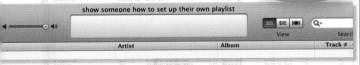

show someone how to set up their own playlist

	Artist	Album	Track #

P.S. Beware of including danceable stuff on the playlists, as this might cause one or both of your parents to spontaneously dance, and someone might see. You have been warned!

WRITE A LETTER TODAY

No, not the ABC kind of letters. That would be too easy. Get a pen and paper, sit right down, and write a letter to someone you know. Fold it up, put it in an envelope, address it, and stick on a stamp. Get yourself down to the nearest mailbox and post it. Done!

BE SOMEONE'S HERO (INE)

You may not be able to fly faster than a speeding bullet or ride to school in an invisible jet, dressed in a cape and identity concealing mask (although, when you think about it, that would be pretty awesome), but you can still become someone's superhero today. If you know of someone in distress, offer your help. Do what you can to make it better.

SHARE YOUR CHOCOLATE BAR

There is one word that makes almost everyone happy. That word is chocolate. Share your chocolate with a friend and double up your happiness.

ORGANIZE A SUMMER CARNIVAL

FOR THE LITTLE KIDS IN THE NEIGHBORHOOD

If you want to bring a lot of smiles to the little kids in your neighborhood, get together with a group of friends and set up a cool summer carnival. With plenty of games, races, and a little sunshine, your family-friendly activity may be the hit of the summer. Here's what to do. Pick your location. You'll need a big open area, either a playing field or park, or someone's yard. Get permission from the owner or city parks department, as needed. Pick a day, make a list of tasks and divide them up, decide what activities you will feature, and get planning. The more you put into it beforehand, the more fun your day will be. Here are some ideas for super-fun games and activities. The rest is up to you!

WATER BALLOON CATCH

Fill up some balloons with water. Get three or more players to stand in a circle and toss a water balloon around until someone gets a silly soaking. As a messy alternative to this, make a small hole in the water balloon before you fill it up, so that it leaks just a trickle of water over everyone.

BALLOON SHAVING

You'll need inexpensive shaving cream, a safety razor (note: not for very young kids), and balloons. Blow up a few balloons and cover them with a coating of shaving cream. Each contestant must try to "shave" the balloon without popping it, and ending up in a shower of shaving cream.

BALLOON BUSTER

Inflate a bunch of balloons and tie one to each player's ankle with a couple of feet of string. At the starting signal, everyone tries to step on and pop the other players' balloons while keeping theirs unpopped. The last person with an intact balloon wins.

THREE-LEGGED RACE

You'll need some bandanas for this. Mark out a finish line. At the starting line, a pair of players will stand side-by-side while you gently tie their two inner legs together just above the ankle. The first pair across the finish line wins.

RADICAL RELAY

Set up a relay race with a twist: each lap must be completed in a different way. For example, in a five-lap relay, contestants can crawl, crab-walk, run backward, do cartwheels, and skip. (Write the order of the laps on a poster board so that everyone knows what to do and when.) The first team to finish the last lap is the winner.

SPONGE SOAKER

You need a clean garbage can lid (or a round plastic disc sled), a clean bucket filled up with water, and three sponges. Pick a lucky parent to be the defender. Each kid has three chances to toss a soaking-wet sponge at the defender, who uses the lid like a shield to bat the sponges away.

SEND A CARE PACKAGE TO A RELATIVE IN COLLEGE

So your brother, sister, cousin, aunt, or uncle made it to college! How cool is that? And why would they want to sign up for more school after 12 straight years of it, not counting kindergarten? Anyway, that's not the point. College is great, but it can be a little tough being away from home, especially in the first year. Sending a care package can help them feel special and remind them of you, the kid back home who is learning to be good. You don't have to spend a lot of money—just think about little things that might make them smile. You can't send perishable stuff, because you never know how long the package might sit around, but almost anything else is good to go. Here is a list of suggestions to inspire you, or you could think up some stuff on your own.

Boredom-busting stuff: a new deck of cards, puzzle books, magazines, paperback books, etc.

Get-out-and-play stuff: a frisbee, jump rope, hacky sack, juggling balls, even kid stuff like squirt guns.

Healthy(ish) snacks: energy bars, dried fruits, nuts and seeds, trail mix, soup mix, microwave popcorn, and if they are far away, a local candy or treat that they can buy only at home. You may want to throw in a few extras of some of these so they can share things.

Useful stuff: coupons, phone cards, gift certificates for movie rentals, food, or shopping, laundry stuff, a roll of quarters, personal care items, stamps, a list of family e-mail addresses and contact numbers (you could buy an inexpensive address book and fill it in.)

Stuff from home: lots and lots of pictures (people, places, and pets), copy of the local newspaper and high school newspaper, letters and notes collected from friends or family, something silly to remind them of home, like a take-out menu from his or her favorite restaurant.

P.S. Make sure you include a letter from you!

SEND A VALENTINE TO A VETERAN

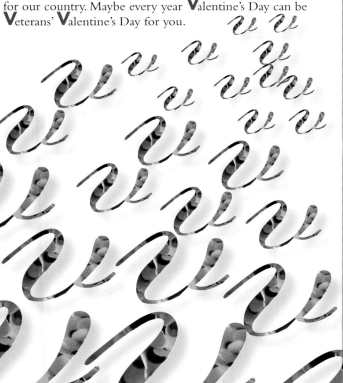

V is not just for Valentines. Valentines are not just for classmates. This year why not Volunteer to send some Valentines to your local Veteran's home? Wouldn't that be a Very nice thing to do? Because Veteran's need our thanks for everything they did for our country. Maybe every year Valentine's Day can be Veterans' Valentine's Day for you.

SEND A GROUP E-MAIL TO A FRIEND WITH LOTS OF PICTURES

It's tough when someone from your gang of friends moves away. You don't know when you'll see them again, or how you will fill that friend-shaped hole in your life. Imagine how rough it must be for them, too. One of the best deeds you could ever do for a friend who's moved away is construct a huge, giant e-mail with a message from everyone who misses them. Ask everyone to do it—it will only take a minute or so. You might even ask a teacher or two to write something. Then attach loads of pictures of the gang, the school, and your old stomping grounds in the neighborhood. Press send, and make his or her day.

TELL SOMEONE WHAT A GREAT JOB THEY DO

Everyone likes to hear nice things like **YOU'RE LOOKING NICE TODAY** or **HEY THAT WAS A COOL WHEELIE**, but it is especially nice to tell someone that they are doing a great job. You could tell your teacher (do not cross your fingers behind your back), your school bus driver, the cafeteria worker, the janitor, the assistant principal, the guidance counselor, the school librarian, or the sports coach. Smile and hand over a nice, fresh compliment.

"A fellow who that count, d usually stop them."

does things

oesn't

to count

Variation of a saying by Albert Einstein

MAKE SOMEONE LAUGH TODAY

Knock, knock!

Who's there?

It's me, with a joke to make you laugh!

Why?

Because it's my good deed for the day.

Who did you say was there again?

Wooden shoe.

Wooden shoe? Wooden shoe who?

Wooden shoe like to hear the joke now?

MAKE A PEN PAL AT THE LOCAL SENIOR CENTER

Have you got the write stuff? No doubt there are plenty of people at your local senior center who would love to have a pen pal—a young whipper-snapper like you. Call the volunteer line and ask if there is someone at the center who would really appreciate some mail. Then drop them a line from time to time—e-mails, a quick letter, a greeting card, even a postcard. It may be the start of a beautiful friendship.

P.S. Don't forget to include a P.S.

HELP AN OLDER PERSON AT THE GROCERY STORE

Even the most convenient of convenience stores may be inconvenient for an older shopper. Products at the top and the bottom of the shelves might be hard to reach, and with all those choices it might be tricky to spot exactly what item you need. If you see someone struggling, please offer to help. Put on your best smile, too. Attention all shoppers! Good deed in aisle three!

PAY SOMEONE'S BUS FARE

When you get on the bus, pay your fare and then pay an extra one, too. Your identity as a good-deed superhero remains hidden, and you may be able to watch someone's surprised smile!

ASK YOUR PRINCIPAL IF YOU CAN MAKE A GOOD DEED ANNOUNCEMENT

How would you like to ask every kid in the school to do a good deed? You'd probably lose your voice before you got even halfway through. However, you could reach them all if you make an announcement over your school PA system. Ask your principal if you can make the announcement. You could say something like: My fellow classmates! Friends, teachers, and countrymen! Lend me your ears! Today is unofficially an official good deed day at our school. I would like to challenge each and every one of you to do a good thing for someone today. If it is true that kindness is contagious, I hope our whole school gets a terrible case of niceness. Thank you for your attention.

P.S. If your voice starts to croak like a frog and you feel incredibly nervous, don't worry. Just imagine you are talking to one other kid, instead of a whole lot of them.

EMPTY THE DISHWASHER

What is that thing in the kitchen…that thing that makes noise and spits out clean dishes? Of course! It's a dishwasher! This incredible machine actually washes up your messy plates and pots and pans and makes them sparkle and shine, as if by magic! However, there is one small catch. Someone does need to unload the dishwasher when the cycle is finished, and put everything away. This someone could be you!

Please sing along

GIVE SOMEONE A HALF-BIRTHDAY CARD

Surprise someone you know with a half-birthday card on their half-birthday (that's birthday minus six months…but you knew that.) You might be the kind of kid who doesn't do good deeds by halves, but this time you'll just have to give in.

P.S. If you want to make them laugh, you could do something silly like cut the card in half, or offer half a cupcake.

TREAT YOUR SISTER LIKE A PRINCESS

Your sister probably went through a big princess phase, or maybe she's still in it. No matter which, she might appreciate a little bit of royal treatment from you. Fluff the pillow before she sits on the couch, ask if you can change the channel for her, offer to bring her a drink or a snack, and so on. She will, of course, be highly suspicious of your motives, but leave her wondering.

PUT THE TOILET SEAT DOWN

Enough said.

HOLD A TEACHER APPRECIATION DAY

An apple for the teacher just doesn't cut it anymore, does it? You might grumble from time to time, and that's normal, but really your teachers deserve a big thank you. They do! So get a group of volunteers together and brainstorm a few ways to show your appreciation. Talk with your principal about your plans. You might consider:

A coffee and bagel morning in the teachers' lounge.

A delicious donut delivery after first period.

Teatime in the afternoon, with cakes and tea.

A make-your-own ice cream sundae party on a hot day.

Hot chocolate (with marshmallows) and cookies on a cold day.

Do you think any of these ideas will sweeten up your teachers? Maybe! But saying thank you in some special way is a very sweet deed indeed.

SHOW SOMEONE A SHORTCUT ON A GAME

Bet you're good to go when it comes to gaming. You've probably racked up more points in your time than a porcupine. (A whole bunch of porcupines.) Did you ever come across a shortcut or hint or cheat that totally changed your game? If so, do the deed thing and pass it along to someone else.

TEACH A CARD GAME TO YOUR LITTLE BROTHER

It's kind of hard to remember in these days of whiz-bang gaming, but once upon a time, in a galaxy not very far away, kids just like you could amuse themselves for hours with a deck of cards. Yes, I know! It seems hard to believe. But playing cards is actually pretty cool. They cost almost nothing, they are completely portable, and you can play games by yourself or with other kids. Learn a couple of games, and you're good to go. To turn this into a good deed, teach your little brother a card game or two. There are games out there for all ages. He will really appreciate the time you spend with him, and he might even let you win a game from time to time. But don't count on it.

PUT A QUARTER IN A PARKING METER THAT IS ABOUT TO EXPIRE

Have you ever seen someone tearing down the street toward his car with a fistful of change, ready to feed the hungry parking meter before the red arrow shows? If you keep a couple of quarters in your pocket, you can do a super-secretive good deed. When you walk by a meter that is creeping toward red, drop in a quarter. You may save someone an expensive parking ticket, and they'll never know who helped them out: the ideal way to do a good deed.

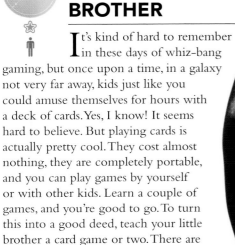

HOLD A NEIGHBORHOOD BARBECUE

How would you like to do a good deed for everyone on your street? Bring your neighbors together with a fantastic potluck barbecue party. To pull it off, you're going to need a lot of help (including adult assistance), a lot of planning, and a lot of ideas. But, guess what? It will be a lot of fun.

After you've discussed this with your parents, pick a date for the big BBQ day. About a month before, start planning. Meet with your friends at your designated BBQ HQ. Divide up areas of responsibility and put someone in charge of each area. Your list of tasks might look something like this:

CEO OF BBQ

LOCATION EXPERT

MVP OF RSVP

OVERALL FOOD GURU

LEMONADE MAGNATE

CHIEF OF PAPER PLATES, NAPKINS, CUTLERY, AND CUPS

KING OF KIDS' ACTIVITIES

MASTER OF LAWN CHAIRS AND TABLES

PREPMASTER AND CLEAN-UP LEADER

Talk through everything you'll need to do. Ask your Location Expert to recommend a site for the picnic. Figure out the food with your Food Guru. You might need to involve a parent here. Since your allowance probably does not stretch to feeding an entire neighborhood, you will need to ask people to bring food donations (hot dogs and veggie dogs, burgers, buns, chips, salsa, dips, soda, ice, salads, potluck dishes, a watermelon or two, etc.). Make lists of what needs to be done way in advance.

When your plan is awesomely clear, get the word out! Create invitations on the computer, and remember all the W's (who, what, where, when, and why.) Include information on what food items you'd like people to bring. Ask people to RSVP your MVP of RSVPs.

In the month leading up to the party, you should be meeting regularly to go over your plan. This is when you report on your progress so far. The Master of Lawn Chairs and Tables, for example, should now have a list of loaners from whom he or she will collect, and the King of Kids' Activities will list the play equipment needed and any activities planned. The CEO of BBQ will secure the services of a fine chef (AKA Dad) to cook on the day.

A couple of days before, run through your lists again to make sure you've got everything. You can never have too much ketchup. When the big day arrives, set up all the tables and chairs, get out the plates, cups, and cutlery, put out non-perishable food items, and set up a kids' play area. Make sure there are places to throw the trash away, and separate containers for things that can be recycled. Ask the chef to get the grill going.

When people arrive, why not hand out those "my name is…" name tags. It's kind of cheesy, but if you're throwing this bash so people can get to know each other, name tags are a great idea. Otherwise, you may never figure out who that guy was who had an orange moustache from eating all the cheese curls.

Then, be the hosts with the most. Try to chat with at least three people you don't know. Keep the hot dogs coming. Thank everyone for coming.

When the last smiley ketchup face has been squirted on to the last burger, when the last ice cube melts into a little puddle, get down to the cleaning.

Raise a glass of lemonade to each other. Your BBQ was Brilliant Beyond Question.

DONATE CHILDREN'S DVDS TO A HOSPITAL OR SHELTER

Now that you're a big kid, some of the movies and cartoons you might have loved when you were little may be lonely and neglected at the back of your DVD collection. Just because you're through with talking mice and animal sidekicks doesn't mean the end for these classics, though. Collect the DVDs and donate them to a children's hospital or a shelter. Ask your family and friends to do the same. Your old favorites are bound to be hits with a whole new audience.

HELP A YOUNGER KID TO CROSS THE STREET

Q. Why did the chicken cross the road?
A. To get to the other side.
Q. Why did the chicken only cross the road halfway?
A. She wanted to lay it on the line.

Enough of the chicken jokes—crossing the street safely is no laughing matter. And if busy traffic is enough to ruffle your feathers sometimes, imagine how scary crossing the road can be for a little kid. Do him a favor and help him across the street. Tell him to stick with you, and he'll be safe. You can explain a little bit about road safety as you cross. Remind him to stop, look, and listen. When you get to the other side, you have earned a good deed. Now that is something to crow about.

BUY A SODA FOR THE PERSON BEHIND YOU IN LINE

So imagine standing in line at the fast-food place, thinking, this line is crazy. It should really be called a slow-food place. Then, imagine when you finally get up to the counter, the nice person working there hands you a soda…free! He says the person in front of you paid for it as a random good deed.

Now imagine all this again, except **YOU** are the person doing the random good deed for the person standing in line behind you.

GOT THAT?

HELP SOMEONE WEED OR PLANT A FLOWER BED OR GARDEN

Do you have a green thumb? Have you seen a doctor? No, seriously, are you handy in the garden? Would you like to do a good deed that enables you to get dirt under your fingernails without having your mother yell at you? OK, then. Here's the deed: ask someone if you can help them do their weeding, or help with the planting of a flower bed or garden. Gardening can be hard work, but with four hands and four green thumbs, the job's done sooner.

P.S. This is an especially nice thing to do for someone who loves their garden, but can't look after it due to illness, etc.

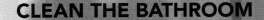

CLEAN THE BATHROOM

Whoa there. No turning the page! Don't try to skip this deed. Sometimes a kid's gotta do what a kid's gotta do, and you've got to clean the bathroom. Your whole family will thank you.

Get the stuff you need: cleaning wipes or spray cleaner suitable for bathroom surfaces, broom, trash bag, toilet cleaner, window cleaner, cleaning cloth or paper towels, and toilet brush. It's best to wear rubber gloves for this deed.

ATTACK THE FLOOR FIRST: PUT THE LAUNDRY IN THE HAMPER. PICK UP TRASH AND TOSS IT. IF THERE ARE TOWELS ON THE FLOOR, HANG THEM UP OR PUT THEM IN THE HAMPER IF THEY'RE DIRTY.

NOW USE A CLEANING WIPE OR SPRAY CLEANER AND A CLOTH TO WIPE DOWN THE BATHTUB, SHOWER STALL, AND SINK. RUB THE SHINY STUFF LIKE THE FAUCET UNTIL IT'S SUPER SHINY. YOUR MOM WILL NOTICE LITTLE THINGS LIKE THAT.

TOILET TIME. SQUIRT IN A LITTLE CLEANER AND SCRUB THE INSIDE OF THE BOWL WITH A TOILET BRUSH. USE ANOTHER WIPE TO GO AROUND THE OUTER SURFACES.

USE WINDOW CLEANER AND A CLOTH TO MAKE THE MIRROR SPARKLE. TAKE A MOMENT TO ADMIRE YOURSELF.

PUT STUFF AWAY IN THE CABINETS OR ON SHELVES SO EVERYTHING LOOKS TIDY, THEN SWEEP THE FLOOR IF NEEDED.

RE-STOCK THE TOILET PAPER.

THAT'S IT! THAT WASN'T SO BAD,

WAS IT?

STEALTH CLEAN THE ENTIRE HOUSE

SUPER VALUE

★ ★
👤 👥

Housework! It has the word "work" in it, doesn't it? (You might have noticed that with homework, too.) Maybe the mere idea of cleaning the whole house makes you absolutely shudder with dread. However, you live in the house, so you should do a little housework. And if you want to make a good deed out of it, why not stealth clean the entire house when your parents are out? Have they ever come back home and said the house looked like a bomb dropped on it? Can you imagine what they will say if the reverse happens, and they come home to a neat and reasonably tidy house? Here's what to do.

First, get all the stuff you need: broom, vacuum cleaner, household cleaners, paper towels or old cloths, and a bucket and mop. You might want to wear rubber gloves.

P.S. This will be a lot easier to do if you can rope in a brother or sister. Then, you can divide up the house into zones and split the work.

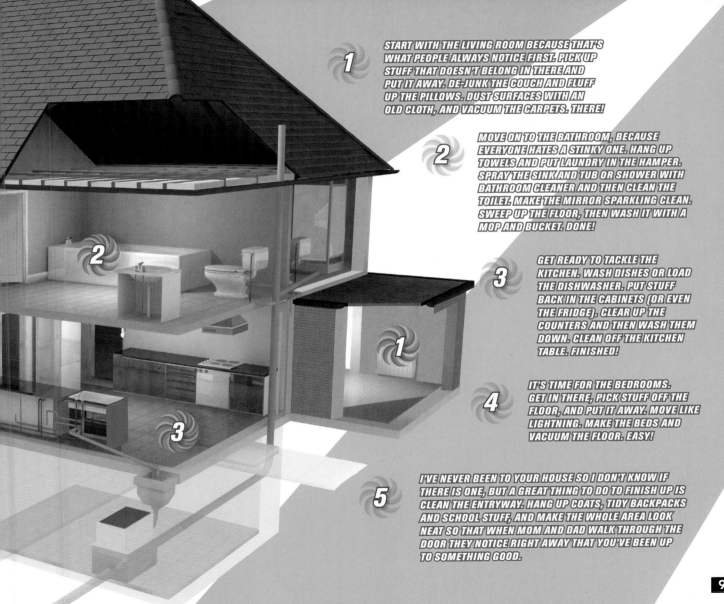

1 START WITH THE LIVING ROOM BECAUSE THAT'S WHAT PEOPLE ALWAYS NOTICE FIRST. PICK UP STUFF THAT DOESN'T BELONG IN THERE AND PUT IT AWAY. DE-JUNK THE COUCH AND FLUFF UP THE PILLOWS. DUST SURFACES WITH AN OLD CLOTH, AND VACUUM THE CARPETS. THERE!

2 MOVE ON TO THE BATHROOM, BECAUSE EVERYONE HATES A STINKY ONE. HANG UP TOWELS AND PUT LAUNDRY IN THE HAMPER. SPRAY THE SINK AND TUB OR SHOWER WITH BATHROOM CLEANER AND THEN CLEAN THE TOILET. MAKE THE MIRROR SPARKLING CLEAN. SWEEP UP THE FLOOR, THEN WASH IT WITH A MOP AND BUCKET. DONE!

3 GET READY TO TACKLE THE KITCHEN. WASH DISHES OR LOAD THE DISHWASHER. PUT STUFF BACK IN THE CABINETS (OR EVEN THE FRIDGE). CLEAR UP THE COUNTERS AND THEN WASH THEM DOWN. CLEAN OFF THE KITCHEN TABLE. FINISHED!

4 IT'S TIME FOR THE BEDROOMS. GET IN THERE, PICK STUFF OFF THE FLOOR, AND PUT IT AWAY. MOVE LIKE LIGHTNING. MAKE THE BEDS AND VACUUM THE FLOOR. EASY!

5 I'VE NEVER BEEN TO YOUR HOUSE SO I DON'T KNOW IF THERE IS ONE, BUT A GREAT THING TO DO TO FINISH UP IS CLEAN THE ENTRYWAY. HANG UP COATS, TIDY BACKPACKS AND SCHOOL STUFF, AND MAKE THE WHOLE AREA LOOK NEAT SO THAT WHEN MOM AND DAD WALK THROUGH THE DOOR THEY NOTICE RIGHT AWAY THAT YOU'VE BEEN UP TO SOMETHING GOOD.

"It isn't the ahead to cli wear you out pebble in yo

mountains
mb that
; it's the
ur shoe."

Muhammad Ali

FIND YOUR OLD BEST FRIEND AND DROP THEM A LINE

☆☆

👤

Do you remember that classic camp-time song:

**Make a new friend but keep the old
One is silver and the other's gold?**

As the campfire crackled and burned, you may have looked around at your circle of friends and thought, there is a lot of gold here. But people move and change and other stuff, and maybe you've lost a couple of solid-gold friends. For this golden deed, find your best friend from kindergarten again, and shoot them an e-mail or letter to say "Hi." It might take a little detective work, but it will be worth it. You may just find yourself a new (old) friend.

LEAVE A BOOK OR MAGAZINE AT THE AIRPORT FOR SOMEONE TO FIND

☆

👤

Sometimes waiting at the airport goes as fast as a jet zooms. But there are other times (plenty of other times) when it feels as if you have waited an eternity, only for another delay to be announced. If you're the kind of person who chills out with a book or magazine, you will probably have plenty of time to finish it while you wait for your flight to be called. When you do, you could leave it in the departure lounge in an obvious place, so that someone else can pass the time with it. Who knows? Maybe your book will go around more times than a luggage carousel.

AFTER A BIG STORM, DROP IN ON OLDER NEIGHBORS

☆

👤

Storms are scary and exciting—thunder so loud you have to cover your ears, lightning streaking across the sky with a huge crackle, and sheets of rain pouring down outside. But of course, storms can be very dangerous. After the thunder rumbles into the distance, the light show stops, and the last raindrop drops, why not check in with your older neighbors (especially if the storm has knocked the power out) and make sure things are OK? It's a good deed and a good idea.

P.S. If the power is out, it would be a storming good idea to take along an extra flashlight and batteries.

PACK YOUR LUNCH (AND YOUR BROTHER'S LUNCH)

Many people say that their favorite class in school is lunch. Are you one of them? If you take your lunch to school, why not give your mom a break one morning and pack it yourself? It's not a chore, and it will give her a little extra time in the morning, which is what parents love. Pack one for your brother or sister, too.

Do not attempt to put a spider in a sibling's lunch. It's not nice to them or to the spider. But here are some good things you could put in:

The basics: you need a source of protein to keep you rocking, complex carbs for energy, calcium for those healthy bones and teeth, and fruit and veggies for all the yummy vitamins and minerals they contain.

Protein: sandwich fillings are key here. Chicken, ham, tuna, cheese, peanut butter, eggs, hummus… whatever floats your boat! (Or fills your bun.)

Carbs: refined carbohydrates give you a burst of energy, but it doesn't last. You need to keep going all day long, so choose complex carbs (whole-wheat bread, or pasta or rice salads) to top up your energy levels and keep them steady.

Calcium: milk, cheese, not-too-sugary yogurt, and smoothies will all help your skeleton stay strong.

Fruit and veggies: add a couple of these for variety. Whole fruit—such as apples and bananas—stands up to a little lunchbox bashing, but you could also cut fruit into chunks and put it in a reusable lidded container. Baby carrots and veggie sticks are always a crunchy treat. Dried fruits are good choices, too.

HELP SOMEONE STUDY FOR A BIG TEST

Sometimes it feels as if schoolwork is a giant mountain you can never get on top of. But if you make a little time for studying every day, you should be able to perform at your peak. Say a friend or family member hasn't even reached the foothills yet, and a big test is hanging over their head like an avalanche. There is only one thing to do: offer to help them study for that test. Cheer them on. Tell them that together you can figure out what needs to be done. Put in the time. No matter what grade they eventually get, you will get an A+ and extra credit for doing such a great good deed.

TEST THE SMOKE ALARMS

These smart little devices really can save lives. Several studies have shown that installing smoke alarms can cut the risk of death by fire in half, which is a good thing. But this is the scary part: studies also estimate that a third of smoke alarms installed are not working, either due to the batteries being dead, or someone removing them when your dad forgot about the toast and filled the house up with smoke. So for this good deed, arm yourself with a fresh package of batteries and a stepladder, and go around the house to press the tester button on each smoke alarm. Get 'em all working and get protected.

HELP A LITTLE DUDE ON THE SKATEBOARD

Remember how tough it was learning how to skateboard? Everything seemed weird, from figuring out what stance to take to making the thing actually move when you wanted it to (and stop when you needed it to.) How could a sport that is so cool make you feel so geeky? If you know a kid who is just starting out, why not offer a few tips to him? You can share some of your own skateboarding experience to help his confidence grow, and soon he'll be brave enough to try some big-kid tricks. It feels good helping someone else feel good about himself, too. Your feet will feel like they've left the ground and you won't even be doing an ollie.

TELL SCHOOL CROSSING GUARDS HOW MUCH YOU APPRECIATE THEM

They're there in the morning when you're still rubbing the sleep from your eyes, making sure everyone gets across the street safely. Then they reappear as if by magic in the afternoon. As sure as the school bell will ring, they'll be there to get everyone back across the street and off home again. (Wonder what school crossing guards do for the rest of the day?) Because you already are a nice person, and getting even nicer by the minute if you are all the way to this page, you probably say hello every day. But today, say hello and thank you. Tell them you really appreciate the job they do and that you are thankful that they are there at the start and at the end of every school day. And cross another good deed off the list.

ORGANIZE A FAMILY GAMING NIGHT

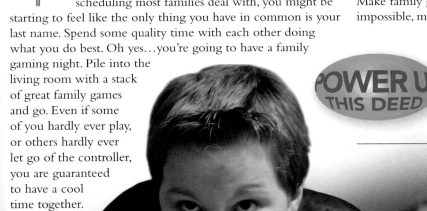

When did you last see your family? Do you kind of, sort of have a distant memory of all being together? What with all the over-scheduling most families deal with, you might be starting to feel like the only thing you have in common is your last name. Spend some quality time with each other doing what you do best. Oh yes…you're going to have a family gaming night. Pile into the living room with a stack of great family games and go. Even if some of you hardly ever play, or others hardly ever let go of the controller, you are guaranteed to have a cool time together. (Plus, your parents are right there, they are hardly going to tell you to shut the game off and do something else for a change.) Who knows, maybe order in some pizza or your favorite takeout tonight? Make family gaming night a regular part of your life, or if that's impossible, meet up on the couch at least once a month.

Some consoles with online gaming will let even far-flung relatives join in the fun. What are you waiting for? Call your Grandma! You never know, she just might get the high score.

POWER UP THIS DEED

"Do the right
gratify some
astonish the

thing. It will

people and

rest."

Mark Twain

LET YOUR BROTHER READ THE COMICS FIRST

Sunday papers! They land on your doormat with a resounding thunk. But if you are a kid, there is only one section you want to get your hands on, and you want to get your hands on it quick: the comics. If your brother is right there alongside you, trying to be first, why not step back, be the good guy that you are, and do a good deed? Hand him the funny papers with a nice smile, and say, "You first! No, I insist."

Then you can get the sports pages before your dad does.

HOLD A LITTLE KID'S HAND IF THEY NEED IT

It's a big old world for little kids sometimes. If the little ones in your life are scared or worried or need a hand to squeeze from time to time, make sure it's yours.

TELL YOUR UNCLE HOW GREAT HE IS

Uncles are cool. They get to pick on your mom or dad without getting grounded. You can always count on them to tell you a goofy story about your mom or dad when they were a kid. So tell your uncle how great he is. You could wait until he falls asleep on the couch, and write "SUPER UNCLE" on his head with a marker. Hmmm, let's skip the marker and just give verbal props.

WHEN SOMEONE FINISHES UNPACKING HIS PURCHASES INTO THE CAR, SECRETLY GRAB THE SHOPPING CART AND RETURN IT

This deed requires a bit of stealth and cunning. So you're in the parking lot of the grocery store, and the person in the car you are approaching has just removed their last shopping bag. Out of nowhere, you appear, and return their cart for them, so they are free to go. You are Shopping-Cart Avenger, superhero of the parking lot! So, check off another good deed.

P.S. Make sure the cart is empty or this will turn from a good deed into a bad one.

MAKE A MOVIE KIT FOR SOMEONE

Sometimes there's nothing more relaxing or entertaining than zoning out in front of a good flick. A couple of hours shutting the world away can do the world of good for your mood.

For this good deed, you will give someone the gift of a DVD (it can be a loaner), but you're going to make it super special by adding in a few inexpensive treats to deliver a real blockbuster of a treat!

First pick the movie, and let it set the theme for you. Be creative! Here are some suggestions just to get you going.

Action/adventure movie: add a couple of bags of microwave popcorn to munch on during the exciting parts, and some long-lasting gum to chew on when the action gets tense. For superhero movies, throw in a couple of comic books and a costume-shop cape as well.

Romantic comedy: some nice chocolates or a single cupcake are a good call here, as well as small beauty treats from the drugstore, like nail polish or an individual face mask. Add the latest issue of a favorite magazine, too.

Classic: for a black-and-white movie, include black-and-white snacks such as crème-filled chocolate sandwich cookies. Specialty candy stores carry vintage brands so you can pick a snack that fits in with the era of the film. Or, link up the snack with the movie location: bagels for New York City, or fortune cookies for a movie set in Chinatown, for example.

Science fiction: Futuristic snacks like Pop Rocks or astronaut ice cream will treat your favorite sci-fi fan. Include a magazine dedicated to sci-fi television and movies. You can also make your own action figure of your friend by printing out a picture of the sci-fi star and replacing its face with a photo of your friend. Glue it onto cardboard and cut it out.

Kid's movies: add some juice boxes and healthy snacks. Homemade popcorn balls are a fantastic addition. For a special treat, include a couple of stickers and coloring or activity books that tie in with the theme of the movie.

To assemble your kit, think about a container to hold the stuff. If you go to the movies, you could ask for an extra popcorn bucket to hold your movie kit. Wrap a kid's kit in the comics section of the newspaper or in "futuristic" aluminum foil for a sci-fi movie.

IF YOU SEE A PENNY...

IF YOU SEE A PENNY PICK IT UP, THE REST OF THE DAY, YOU'LL HAVE GOOD LUCK. BUT IF YOU SEE A PENNY AND PICK IT UP, THEN DONATE THAT PENNY AND KEEP IT UP BECAUSE LOTS OF PENNIES SOON ADD UP.

COLLECT MITTENS

Little hands need little mittens when the temperature drops below freezing. If you want to do a lot of good, organize a mitten drive in your community. You could set up a donation box in a place where lots of people come and go (like the library or school). You might want to start a mitten tree (attaching pairs of mittens to a sturdy tree with clothespins) in the center of town. When you've collected the mittens, donate them to a local charity or shelter. Warm hands lead to warm hearts.

P.S. Gloves are OK, too. And hats. And scarves.

MEET WITH YOUR PRINCIPAL AND ASK HOW YOU CAN HELP

Do you remember the difference between "principle" and "principal"? One of them is something you stand for, the other is that guy or lady who stands at the front of the auditorium in school...but which is which? You probably remember that the "principal" is your "pal." (These cool little memory tricks are called mnemonics, by the way. Know any more?) So, if you want to show your principal that you are a kid with principles, ask for a meeting. Be respectful and polite. Tell him or her all about the good deeds you are doing in this book, and ask if there is any way to do good stuff for the school, too. Your principal will be impressed with your principles, and may offer you some great opportunities to make a difference at your school.

SET UP A LEMONADE STAND

Nothing beats the summer heat like an ice-cold glass of lemonade. And a street-corner lemonade stand makes everyone happy. Pick a perfect spot, mix up a tasty citrusy blend that's like summer in a cup, and you'll end the day with a box full of quarters. So how do you turn lemons into good deeds? That's easy. Pick your favorite local charity and make a big sign for your lemonade stand to say:

Fresh
LEMONADE
All proceeds from today's lemonade sale will go to _____ to help them with their good work.
SO DRINK UP AND TIP GENEROUSLY!

HELP SOMEONE IN YOUR FAMILY FIGURE OUT HOW TO USE THE COMPUTER

You may find it impossible to imagine, but there was a time when computers filled up entire rooms. How's that for weird? (They have a really fascinating history, you should look it up…on the computer.) Anyway, most of us are pretty good with computers because we've grown up with them at home and school. But there are probably some people in your family (no names mentioned) who would struggle with turning the thing on, let alone using it. Sit down and show them the ropes (or should that be cables?). Go slowly, one step at a time. Remember, people pick up stuff at different speeds. Offer to be on call in case they need help. There! You've done another good thing. Before too long, the new computer whiz will be posting your baby pictures up on line for everyone to admire.

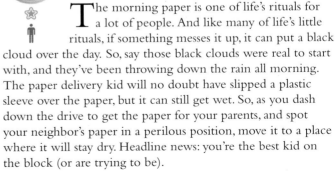

MOVE YOUR NEIGHBOR'S PAPER OUT OF THE RAIN

The morning paper is one of life's rituals for a lot of people. And like many of life's little rituals, if something messes it up, it can put a black cloud over the day. So, say those black clouds were real to start with, and they've been throwing down the rain all morning. The paper delivery kid will no doubt have slipped a plastic sleeve over the paper, but it can still get wet. So, as you dash down the drive to get the paper for your parents, and spot your neighbor's paper in a perilous position, move it to a place where it will stay dry. Headline news: you're the best kid on the block (or are trying to be).

HELP A NEIGHBORHOOD KID TO MAKE A SNOWMAN

How cool is it to wake up on the morning after a big snowstorm and see the whole neighborhood transformed into a winter wonderland? Can it get any better? Yes, it can, when you find out it's a snow day and there is no school. You have the whole day ahead of you to get out there and play in all that white stuff. Do a great deed while you're out there, and teach a little kid your super secret snowman-building skills. As long as there's enough snow, and it's the kind that packs easily in your hand, you are good to go. Here are the basics:

Get mittens and gloves on! You might have noticed that it's cold outside. Talk your young friend through each step as you do it.

Make a snowball. Make it bigger. Keep packing on the snow until you can't hold it easily.

Put the snowball down on the ground and roll it away from you so it picks up more snow as it rolls. Pack down the new snow.

Keep on rolling and packing until you have a giant snowball that is the size you want for the base of your snowman. Roll it into position.

Then, make a slightly smaller ball for the middle, and carefully sit it on top of the bottom ball.

Finally, make the head. You can make the snowman more stable by packing a little extra snow between the layers.

At last, your snowman is ready for some finishing touches. You can give him a face with pebble eyes and a carrot nose. Break off the bottom of a candy cane to give him a stripy smile. You could make hair with some garden twine, or throw on a hat and scarf. Add stick arms, and put a pair of old gloves on the ends. Give him as much personality as you can!

OFFER TO HELP AN OLDER PERSON PUT UP HOLIDAY DECORATIONS

Whatever holidays you celebrate, it's always exciting when your parents get the box of decorations out, and you put them up around the house together. Many families have collections of decorations that may even be older than you are, believe it or not. But if you have a family friend who is elderly and living alone, perhaps they may not be able to put up their holiday decorations. Perhaps they need a little extra help. That's where you come in. Offer to help them do a little decorating. Have a nice long talk while you are at it. Now that's the holiday spirit!

 Make sure that your offer to help put up decorations also includes a promise to come help take them down and put them away. Double deed!

Before

After

SLIP AN ANONYMOUS NOTE INTO SOMEONE'S LOCKER

It's nice to find something good in your locker, something that isn't an old peanut butter sandwich or a gym sock. So if you see someone do a good thing, or someone gives a particularly good answer in class, write a note to him or her and slide it into their locker. Don't sign your name or anything…keep it anonymous. Hopefully your note will not land on a gym sock, and will make someone happy.

GO TO YOUR LITTLE BROTHER'S LITTLE LEAGUE GAME

Is your little brother a sports nut? Does he practically fall asleep with his baseball glove on? Do you suspect that more than 78.2 percent of his waking thoughts are about baseball? Show him how proud you are of him by getting down to his next game, parking your rear on the bleachers, and cheering him on. Everyone needs a fan club, and you can be his.

TEACH A KID ABOUT THE SUN AND PLANETS

The night sky is a pretty awesome sight. It's almost better than watching TV, isn't it? What's up there exactly? Do you think there might be another galaxy where an alien about your age is looking down at you? (You can wave to it, if you want.) Be a star in your own right by teaching a kid everything there is to know about the stars and planets.

There's a whole universe to see and learn about. There is plenty of information about the solar system in books or online. You can buy or download cool star maps that will help you spot and name the constellations, depending on where you live and what time of year it is. Use binoculars to look at the night sky, and consider picking up an inexpensive telescope from an auction site or garage sale. You'll really be amazed. But remember, it is dangerous to look at the Sun through a telescope or binoculars—never do it.

SOME AMAZING PLANET FACTS

- If you drove a car at 60 miles an hour without stopping it would take you 170 years to reach the Sun.
- A day on Mercury is longer than its year.
- On Venus you would see the Sun rise in the West and set in the East.
- Mars has a huge volcano, Olympus Mons, the biggest in the solar system.
- Jupiter is larger than all the other planets put together.
- Saturn has seven major rings and at least 60 moons.
- Uranus revolves sideways.
- On Neptune, one season lasts 40 years.
- Pluto has been downgraded to a "dwarf planet."

YOU
ARE
HERE

DELIVER A TALL GLASS OF ICED TEA ON A HOT DAY TO SOMEONE WORKING OUTSIDE

When the sun beats down relentlessly on a super-hot day and you feel like you could not only fry eggs on the sidewalk, but cook an entire breakfast, spare a thought for the people who have to work outdoors. All work is thirsty work when you've got to be out in the sun. So whether it's mom mowing the lawn, dad fixing the garage door, or your neighbor weeding his garden, deliver a tall, cold glass of delicious iced tea, clinking with ice cubes. And a smile!

PAINT YOUR LITTLE SISTER'S TOENAILS

Anyone who's lived with a little sister knows they go through a phase when they adore nail polish, especially the kind with a couple of handfuls of glitter thrown in. Nail polish is not only smelly, it is messy and can cause a disaster in the house if it spills. So, this is kind of a double good deed. If you offer to paint your little sister's toenails, your parents will be happy because someone older has a grip on the gloopy nail polish. Your sister will be happy because she's going to get the glittery tootsies she so admires. That's two good reasons to paint 10 little toes, and complete yet another good deed.

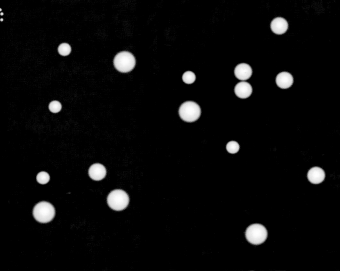

ON A SUMMER NIGHT, CATCH FIREFLIES IN A JAR WITH SOMEONE

Fireflies are cool characters. By day, you'd hardly look twice at them. But at night, when their abdomens flash and twinkle in the summer air, you can't take your eyes off them. So, get a friend, a butterfly net, and a clean screw-top jar with air-holes poked in the lid. Now try to catch fireflies. You can use a flashlight to mimic their signals to attract them to you, or you can just chase them. They are surprisingly tricky to catch, but it is surprisingly fun. Transfer the fireflies to the jar, but only for an hour or so. Then, let them go free.

P.S. It's super fun to catch them in your hands but this increases the risk of squishing, which is not a good deed.

KEEP AN EXTRA PENCIL IN YOUR BACKPACK TO LEND TO A FRIEND

If you see someone scrabbling around frantically in their backpack looking for a pencil (when do you think was the last time they cleaned that out anyway?), calmly unzip your pack, and withdraw the Special Pencil you are keeping there for just this moment. Hand said pencil over to your friend with a smile, and let them know it's free. Pencil yourself in for another good deed.

P.S. This deed counts only if the pencil is sharpened.

SHARE YOUR SNACK AT RECESS

It can feel like an extremely long time between breakfast and your first break at school. You might even worry that your grumbling stomach is going to drown out the teacher's voice. Have no fear, soon recess will be here, and you'll have a chance to munch down on a snack. To turn this into a good deed, simply split your snack in half and share it with someone. Keep the smaller piece for yourself, and give your friend the larger one, because that is the kind of kid you are.

P.S. Do not attempt this with individual grapes, for example.

GIVE SOMEONE A SHOULDER TO CRY ON

If someone you care about is feeling like the weight of the world is on their shoulders, it might all get to be too much sometimes. Let them know that you've got a shoulder (or two) to cry on. Lend them an ear. Give them a hand. Whatever they need, let them know that all they need to do, is ask.

IF YOU USE ALL THE TOILET PAPER, REPLACE IT WITH A NEW ROLL

Don't leave a sad little cardboard tube behind. Recycle the tube by putting it in the correct recycling bin. Then put a fresh new roll of toilet paper on the dispenser and make sure there are new rolls handy for next time. That was easy wasn't it? And you can check off another good deed.

4U
Save the last lollipop for your sister

You like candy. Your sister likes candy. Your sister likes the same candy you like. You have a lollipop. Your sister does not have a lollipop. You are down to your very last lollipop. You really want that lollipop, but give it to your sister instead. Good deed complete! Sweet!

MAKE UP AN EMOTICON FOR SOMEONE

It's hard to believe, but emoticons have been around for more than a hundred years! I know what you're thinking…messaging and texting so did not happen a hundred years ago, LOL! That's true, but an operator's manual for Morse Code more than a hundred years old indicated that the number 73 could stand in for "love and kisses." Surprising, or what?

Anyway, you probably sprinkle these little faces throughout your messages, but why not put your thinking cap on and try to create a special emoticon for a friend. You could try to capture their image, or just make a face that shows how you feel about them, like the one below. They will ROTFL when they take a peek.

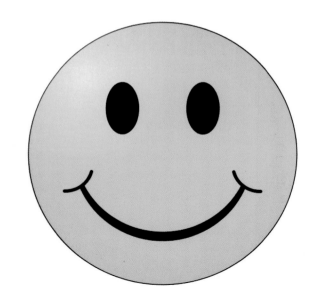

GIVE FLOWERS TO YOUR FAVORITE CASHIER AT THE GROCERY STORE

If you're like most people, you tend to go to the same grocery store all the time. There are probably a few familiar faces among the people who work there. You might even have a favorite cashier. Why not give him flowers (or some candy, or another small gift) and thank him very much for all the great service? You will definitely surprise him. He might even try to scan your bouquet and put it with your shopping!

WHEN THE CLOCKS GO FORWARD OR BACK, CHANGE THEM

Spring forward, fall back. That's the way to remember how the clocks change during daylight saving time. Go into each room and check every time-keeping device. Computers usually reset themselves, but cell phones, microwaves, and ovens, for instance, might need help. If you don't have the instructions, you can usually find out what to do on the Internet.

P.S. It should take you less than an hour, which is what you have already lost or gained.

WRITE A NOTE FOR YOUR MOM AND LEAVE IT ON THE BATHROOM MIRROR

Mirror, mirror on the wall
Who's the fairest of them all?
That would be your mother.
Write her, then, and tell her so,
Put it on a Post-it note®,
Cause there could be no other.

SET UP A SIDEWALK-CHALK ART SHOW

From soap bubbles to squirt guns, there is some summer stuff you never grow out of. One of the coolest summertime classics is sidewalk chalk. Bringing dull gray concrete to life with colorful chalk doodles and drawings can be a blast. It's like being a graffiti artist, but legal! For this deed, pick up a few tubs of inexpensive sidewalk chalk, and get all the kids in the neighborhood together. Give each kid one square of sidewalk to decorate exactly as he or she likes. Even little kids can get involved. You'll bring a lot of color to the neighborhood (until it rains, at least) and also have fun hanging out and being creative together.

SEND HOLIDAY CARDS TO FAMILIES IN A SHELTER

Holiday cards brighten up the house when it's time to celebrate. Sending a card to a friend or relative can be a very good deed indeed. (And if you recycle your cards when the holiday's over, you have done another good deed.) But while loads of cards may spill out of your mailbox at holiday time, there are people who may not have any. So, for each holiday greeting you send, why not send another to a family in a local shelter? You could also do this as a classroom activity. Spread the joy this holiday season.

HELP SOMEONE WITH A CRAFT PROJECT

Sometimes a woodwork or other craft assignment can feel like an anvil hanging over your head by a sliver of thread. It can take a lot of time and preparation, but it's fun once you get started. The longer that you put it off, the more the thread seems to unravel. If you have a friend who is under the anvil, then help him get on with his project. Encourage him to name the time and place, and get to work. Using sharp tools can be daunting, but if two of you work together it will reassure him—and it will be a lot safer. Your crafty heroics will earn you another good deed.

START A SHOPPING LIST ON THE FRIDGE

Isn't it terrible when you really, REALLY crave a peanut butter and jelly sandwich, and you open the fridge to get the peanut butter, and someone, SOMEONE has scraped out all but the tiniest, most minuscule amount of peanut butter that would not even make a sandwich for an ant, and then returned the jar to the fridge without telling anyone? (Hopefully that person was not you, but if it was, you are about to get a reprieve.) To prevent a terrible peanut-butter related crisis and do a good deed for the whole family at the same time, make a grocery list and attach it to the fridge door with a magnet. When you use the last of something, dispose of its container properly and then note it down on the list. Next time someone goes to the market, it will be a cinch to grab the list and replenish depleted peanut-butter stockpiles. Phew!

WELCOME NEW STUDENTS TO THE SCHOOL

There is nothing so terrifying as walking through the school doors on the first day at a new school. You must have done that a couple of times. Remember all the thoughts that went through your head? Will anyone like me? Will I do something embarrassing that everyone will remember for the rest of the year? Will I ever remember my locker combination? Imagine how nice it would have been if a friendly person walked up to you, welcomed you to the school, and told you to come and find them if you had any questions, no matter how strange, at all, ever! (Do you get the feeling there is a good deed coming?) Make sure you are that welcoming person. You could even get together with a group of friends and set yourself up as the Official Unofficial School Welcome Group (that's the OUSWG to you).

WRITE AN INSPIRATIONAL MESSAGE AND PASS IT ON

You've got to be a little bit brave to do this deed, but go on—give it a try. Think of an inspiring phrase or quote. Use the Internet to find one if you aren't feeling particularly inspired. Write it down on a piece of paper, and then (here is the brave part) give it to a stranger. It's sort of like a fortune cookie without the cookie part. You might make someone's day.

"When it comes to giving, some people stop at nothing."

Anonymous

TEACH SOMEONE TO DO A CANNONBALL DIVE

Come on in, the water's fine! Is there anything cooler than a pool on a hot summer day? And is there any cooler way to get yourself in that pool, than making a gigantic splash with the perfect cannonball dive? It's a time-honored, kid-approved tradition. And if you show someone else how to do a cannonball, you'll make a good deed splash. Here's the way to tell 'em how to do the dive: make sure the water is deep enough for diving. Step back from the edge of the pool so you can get a running start. Make sure the area between you and the pool is clear and not slippery, then dash to the edge of the pool and jump as high as you can. Tuck your body into a ball, with your knees up to your chest and your arms wrapped around them. Tuck your chin down, hold your breath, and get ready to make an enormous splash. Screaming like a banshee is optional. (Some community and public pools prohibit this dive. If you are swimming in one of them, then DON'T do a cannonball and collect a good deed point, anyway, for following the rules.)

SEND AN E-CARD TO SOMEONE

Surprise someone today with an e-card personalized just for her. There are lots of free sites online that enable you to create a custom-made greeting. With a few clicks you can find something that will be the perfect fit for your friend.

fold
over

E-CARD

ADDRESS

MESSAGE

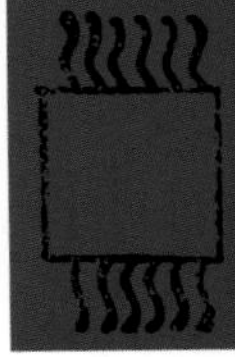

(GET IT? THIS IS AN
E-SHAPED CARD)

fold
over

IF YOUR FAMILY WANTS TO GET A PET, ADOPT A SHELTER PET

Why adopt an animal from a shelter? Paws and think about it a moment. Adopting an animal from a shelter makes sense. Shelter pets have health checks and shots, and may be housebroken already. There are rescue groups for those purebred animals, too. So don't bark up the wrong tree. Use an animal shelter.

P.S. Warning! Do not attempt to do this on your own. Make sure you have permission from your parents or you'll be in the doghouse!

SEND A POSTCARD TO YOUR PARENTS WHEN ON A TRIP

Wait a second. Your parents are right there with you, aren't they? Why on earth would you send a postcard to them? And, duh, no one is at home to get the mail, either.

But wait. When you are on vacation, secretly buy a postcard and address it to your parents. On the back, tell them how much fun you are having, and thank them for taking you to such cool places. Say you appreciate them spending time with you. Then get sneaky and mail it home.

When you return, your parents will find this thank-you postcard and marvel at what a good kid you are.

BLOW BUBBLES FOR LITTLE KIDS TO POP

Blow bubbles? No troubles. It's hard to believe that something so simple and inexpensive can capture a little kid's attention completely. But soap bubbles are pretty much irresistible, as is the urge to pop them with little fingers. Next time you are in the drugstore or discount store, splurge on a tub of bubble liquid. (You can also make your own if you are the crafty type.) When little kids are around, fill the air with bubbles and enjoy a good feeling that is impossible to pop.

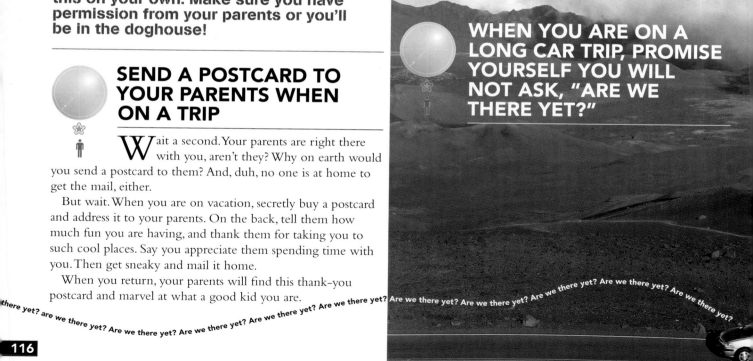

WHEN YOU ARE ON A LONG CAR TRIP, PROMISE YOURSELF YOU WILL NOT ASK, "ARE WE THERE YET?"

there yet? are we there yet? Are we there yet? Are we there yet? Are we there yet? Are we there yet? Are we there yet? Are we there yet? Are we there yet? Are we there yet? Are we there yet?

MAKE A HEART-SHAPED PIZZA FOR YOUR FAMILY ON VALENTINE'S DAY (OR ANY DAY)

Nothing says "love" like a heart. And nothing says "love" to your stomach like a pizza. Combine the two, and you have the perfect way to say "I love you" to your family on Valentine's day: a delicious heart-shaped pizza. Here's how to make it.

WHAT YOU NEED:

A package of ready-to-use pizza dough (plain or whole-wheat)

Flour to keep it from sticking to everything

A jar of pizza topping or tomato sauce

Shredded mozzarella or Italian-mix cheese (or any other cheese you like)

All the toppings your family loves: pepperoni, ham, sausage, ground beef, fresh veggies, garlic, olives, hot peppers, you name it!

A super-hot 450-degree oven (be extremely careful here)

Pizza pan or pizza stone

WHAT TO DO:

Sprinkle a little flour on a cutting board, unwrap the dough, and let it sit for half an hour or so. You can skip this part, but it makes some pizza dough taste better. Then get the oven cranked up. Sprinkle your palms with a little flour. Now begin shaping the dough, pushing it down and stretching it out until you make a heart shape. Try to keep the dough the same thickness all over so it cooks evenly.

Do not throw it up in the air like the chefs at the pizza place do unless you want it to be stuck to the ceiling, which is not a Good Deed. Lay it out on a pan. Squeeze the edges to build up a rim of dough to hold in the toppings. Use the back of a spoon to spread a thin layer of sauce across the dough. Sprinkle on the grated cheese, and top with all the pizza toppings you love. Bake for about 10 to 15 minutes. Serve to the ones you love.

"If you haven'
in your heart,
worst kind of

t any charity
you have the
heart trouble."

Bob Hope

JOIN THE ANIMAL ADOPTION PROGRAM AT THE LOCAL ZOO

Have you ever wanted a pet tiger? Or, a flock of real flamingos in the front yard instead of the plastic ones? Or, for those of you who live in tall buildings, your own giraffe? Well, you can't do any of those things, but you can support your local zoo and do a very good deed for a furry, feathery, scaly, slimy, or fuzzy animal of your choice by joining an animal sponsorship program. (You could do this as a class project; ask your teacher.) Your sponsorship money goes toward buying supplies, treats, and toys for your chosen animal, and the zoo may reward your good deed with a photograph, biography, fact sheet, and maybe even a zoo discount so you can come and meet your animal friend. So go on, be a monkey's uncle! Sort of.

MAKE AN EASTER BASKET FOR YOUR PARENTS

That Easter Bunny guy thinks of everyone, doesn't he? Hopping all over the place, leaving chocolate treats in baskets. Just how does he do that? Bet that bunny hops right past your mom and dad, though. Do they get a basket brimming with delicious goodies? Probably not. For this good deed, you are going to become your parents' personal Easter Bunny. Buy a small basket and some treats, and keep them hidden. On Easter morning, get up early, fill the basket with treats, and leave it outside their door, or on the kitchen table. Adding a homemade card is a nice touch. Then hop away quickly, secure in the knowledge that you have done a good deed.

LEND SOMEONE LUNCH MONEY

No one likes forgetting their lunch money. So if you see someone at school looking very frustrated (and hungry), dig deep. Offer to loan him or her enough money for lunch. (Or let them use your swipe card, if your school uses them.) Your good deed will not only fill a hole in his or her stomach, it will also fill a hole in your good-deed to-do list.

P.S. If there is Mystery Meat on the menu this good deed might backfire.

MAKE SOME TOYS FOR YOUR DOG OR CAT

☆☆

Your pet has given you a lot of fun times. Why not reward the little critter with some homemade toys? Pets love to play, and the exercise is good for them. Here are a few ideas.

IDEAS FOR CATS:

Cut the fingertips out of an old glove, stuff with cotton or fabric scraps, and sew shut. Add a long "tail" of fabric or yarn. If you like, use a simple cross-stitch to make eyes. You have made a marvelous mousie.

Ping-pong balls are excellent cat toys.

Tie a feather, a pom-pom, or a small lightweight toy to a small length of thin wooden doweling with string or dental floss. You have made a cat-fishing pole. See what you can catch.

IDEAS FOR DOGS:

Find 3 or 4 socks that no longer have matches or have more holes than Swiss cheese. Roll up all but the longest sock. Stuff them inside it, and tie a knot above the stuffed area. Double the sock over the entire ball and knot again. Keep on doing this until you can't make any more knots. Cut off any excess. Don't let your dog chew on this, as bits of sock can harm him, but he will love playing catch with it.

Many baby toys make excellent dog toys. Look at garage sales to pick up a few inexpensive treats for your four-legged friend.

If you find an old garden hose at a garage sale, you can ask an adult to help you cut it into lengths to make doggie chew toys. They float, too, so you can toss them into water for a wet game of catch.

DELIVER SOUP TO SOMEONE WITH THE SNIFFLES

AaaaaaCHOO! Has your friend got an itchy nose and a scratchy throat brought on by a yucky cold? She needs warm wishes and a great big bowl of steaming-hot soup. Soup sometimes is the best medicine when someone is feeling under the weather. It's even OK if it comes from a can, because the thought is from the heart. Deliver her favorite kind of steaming hot soup (in a thermos jar) to her door. This is room service of the nicest kind.

Add a box of tissues and a get-well card, and show how much you care.

KEEP YOUR FAMILY AND FRIENDS CONNECTED

It can be pretty tough keeping track of everyone you know. You are never going to be able to memorize all those numbers: home numbers, cell phone numbers, and work numbers. Then there are e-mail addresses and regular addresses, birthdays and regular days. Even an elephant (which never forgets) would be perplexed. So one day, sit down at the computer, and compile a master list of all your family addresses and contact numbers. (You could do the same with your friends.) Style it so that it's easy to read and use, proofread it and fix any errors, then send a copy to everyone on the list. People will really appreciate having all this info in one handy, dandy place. Now all you need to figure out is how you got related to some of those people anyway....

GIVE UP YOUR SEAT IN A CROWDED AIRPORT LOUNGE OR BUS STATION

No one likes waiting around for a plane or a train, and there are never enough places to sit in the waiting area. If you are lucky enough to snag a seat, then you are sitting pretty, but keep your eyes open for someone who needs it more than you: people less able to stand, older folks, a pregnant woman or someone with little kids, someone loaded down with stuff—you get the idea. Be an outstanding kid and offer your seat.

CLEAN YOUR SISTER'S HAMSTER CAGE

Now, we are not implying here that your sister lives in a hamster cage, or indeed, that your sister is a hamster. Let's say instead that she has a hamster, and that the little fella lives in a nice cage that gets a tiny bit messy and smelly sometimes. Your sister is a responsible pet owner and all that, but it is a chore cleaning out the cage so the hamster can only make it messy again. (Ask your mom if this sounds familiar at all, in relation to your room.) So, do her (and her hamster) a good deed and clean out the hamster home for her. Give the hamster some fresh water, a clean food dish, and nice new bedding to snuggle in.

P.S. Make sure that you put the hamster somewhere safe while you clean the cage, or else this good deed has the potential to go very wrong.

MAKE YOUR SISTER AND HER FRIENDS A ROUND OF ROOT BEER FLOATS

Nothing quite wets the whistle like a root beer float. It's a drink and a dessert all in one! Next time your sister has her friends around, treat them to a trayful of these delicious frosty treats. Just put a scoop or two of vanilla ice cream in a tall glass, and fill up the glass with root beer (or cola). Add a straw and a long-handled spoon, and present your fabulous frosty floats to your sister's gang. Mmmmm-my!

P.S. Make one for yourself, too (with an extra scoop of ice cream).

SEND LETTERS TO A FRIEND WHO IS AWAY AT SUMMER CAMP

Dear Friend,

Hi! How's it going up there at camp? Is your bunk bed only a little less lumpy than the oatmeal they make you eat for breakfast? Are the mosquitoes the size of hummingbirds like last year? Are the other kids in your cabin fun, or have they recently been released from reform school? Do your ears still ring everytime someone starts singing Kumbyah? Did you flip your canoe and take an unscheduled bath in the lake again, while everyone laughed?

So many questions!

Things here aren't the same without you. I can't wait to hear about your summer, and to tell you about mine.

See you very soon,
Your best friend

TELL YOUR BIG BROTHER OR SISTER HOW MUCH YOU ADMIRE HIM OR HER!

Do you look up to an older sibling? Is that just because they are taller than you are? But seriously, there are probably lots of things to admire about your brother or your sister. Really! No, really, there are. Honest. Come on. Lots. When you figure out the best one, the one that makes you proudest to be related to them, then tell them!

HELP A NEIGHBOR RAISE THE FLAG ON THE 4TH OF JULY

Long may Old Glory wave, especially on the holiday that celebrates the independence of the United States of America. Many people like to display the American flag on the 4th of July, so for this good deed, offer your flag-hoisting skills to a neighbor. Always remember that the flag is an important symbol of our nation and the people who fought to protect it, so treat the Stars and Stripes with a great deal of respect. You can find the flag code online if you need a refresher course on how to handle the flag carefully.

P.S. Double the deed by offering to take the flag down, and fold it properly afterward.

CLEAN OUT THE AQUARIUM AND MAKE SOME FISH HAPPY

Don't let your aquarium get so grubby that you can't see your fishy finned friends anymore. After all, how would you like to live in a messy room? (Maybe you shouldn't answer that, depending on the current state of your bedroom.) Get in there and do some cleaning. Carefully move the fish (with some of their tank water) out of the way to a secure location. Scrub up the aquarium walls, rocks and gravel, and any props. (If props are really dirty, rinse them under a warm tap and air dry.) You can buy a siphon tool from the pet store to help you sweep away debris. Clean the filter and hood, too. You should aim to remove about half of the water from the tank as you clean and replace it with clean water (treated with chlorine remover) that is as close to the temperature of the remaining tank water as you can get. Replace everything and run the filter for a bit before you return the fish to their clean home.

Hello! Are there any fish in there?

"A Scout is ne
surprise; he
what to do w
unexpected

ver taken by

knows exactly

hen anything

happens."

ON MY HONOR
I WILL DO MY BEST."

BOY SCOUTS
OF AMERICA

3¢ UNITED STATES POSTAGE

Robert Baden-Powell

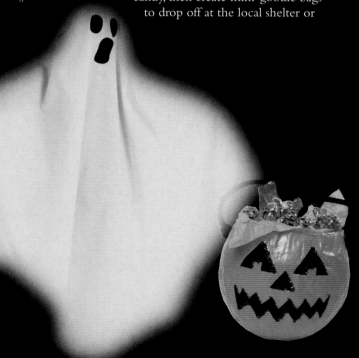

BUY EXTRA HALLOWEEN CANDY AND FILL UP GOODIE BAGS

It's spooky, the amount of candy you can get through on Halloween, isn't it? But this trick-or-treat season, make sure to stock up on extra Halloween candy, then create mini-goodie bags to drop off at the local shelter or children's hospital. Why not make the bags as part of a class project? Use clear plastic bags dressed up with orange and black ribbon or holiday stickers, or purchase Halloween-themed treat bags. It's scarily easy to do.

WRITE A LETTER TO A FAVORITE TEACHER TO SAY THANKS

An apple for the teacher is one thing, but a fantastic letter to thank your very favorite teacher is better than a whole tree full of apples. Plan your letter carefully. Think of specific examples from your time in your teacher's class—a challenging assignment or an inspirational class lesson, for example—and explain why they still mean something to you today. Thank your teacher for teaching you, and, THIS IS VERY IMPORTANT, make sure all your spelling and grammar are OK. (Teachers are fussy about those things.) It's nice to hand-write the letter rather than e-mail it, for a special touch. This deed will take you directly to the head of the class.

SWEEP UP AND WASH YOUR FRONT PORCH

Maybe you have a welcome mat that says "WELCOME" but nothing really says welcome, hello, come on in, like a clean front porch. So, get out the broom and sweep away dust, cobwebs, and debris, then wash off the porch with a squirt from the garden hose or a couple of buckets of water. Presto! Then, make a clean getaway.

AMAZE A LITTLE KID

MAKE SHADOW ANIMALS

You need a flashlight, a wall, and your hands...that's all...to create a menagerie of shadow animals. Awesome!

PULL YOUR THUMB OFF

Practice this in front of a mirror. Hold your left hand out so that all your fingers touch and are in a straight line. Bend the top of your thumb down. Now bend the top of your right thumb down and hold it so it looks as if it's the top of your left thumb. Cover the place they meet with your pointer and middle fingers. Now tell the kid that you are going to pull the top of your thumb off. Slide your left hand to the right while making a terrible face. Ouch!

RUBBER PENCIL TRICK

Wiggle a pencil and make it look as if it's made of rubber. This is another trick that needs plenty of practice in front of a mirror. Hold a pencil between your thumb and index finger, about a third of the way from the tip. Keep your grip loose. Then move your hand up and down, getting faster. Move your arm, not just your wrist.

Little kids already look up to big kids. After all, they are taller. But if you want to surprise, amaze, or even amuse a kid in your life (cousin, sister, brother, niece, or nephew), here are a few tricks of the trade...

The pencil will appear to bounce up and down like a bendy rubber one. Amazing!

MAKE A PAPER STRAW WRAPPER WRIGGLE

Open one end of a dry, paper-wrapped straw and scrunch the wrapper down to the other end. Then push it onto a dry tabletop. Tell the kid you can make it wriggle like a worm. Then put a couple of drops of water or soda onto the paper. As the paper soaks up water and expands, it wriggles!

GUESS THE CARD TRICK

Fan out a deck of cards and ask the kid to pick one. Once he has chosen, start babbling to distract him. Ask him to make sure he has memorized his choice. Tell him to double-check. While he isn't concentrating, turn the deck over and flip the bottom card so that it is back-out, not face-out. Hold the tricked-out deck out to him and ask him to put his card back in the deck. Then start yakking again. Ask him to think very hard about his card as you

quickly turn the deck so it is top-up again. Fan out the cards one more time…his card will be face up, every time!

BECOME A MIND-READER

You need a helper for this trick and at least three other people, plus three envelopes, paper, and pencils. Before you perform the trick, ask your helper to write the word "cat" (or any word you both agree on) on the paper. Then, tell the kids that you can read their minds. Give out envelopes and paper, and tell them to write down a word on the paper, put it in the envelope, and seal it. Collect the envelopes, remembering which one came from each person. Put your helper's envelope at the bottom. Then pretend to concentrate. Say ("Helper's name"), my supreme mind powers have deduced that the word on your paper is ("say agreed word")! Open the envelope on TOP of the stack and read what is on it, but SAY, "Why yes, I

was right!" You can now amaze the next person by "guessing" the word you have read. Repeat until everyone is amazed!

DISAPPEARING SALT SHAKER

This is a great trick to do at a restaurant. You need a nickel, a salt shaker, and a napkin. Tell everyone that you can make the nickel disappear by rubbing it with the salt shaker. Lay the coin on the table. Cover the salt shaker with the napkin and pick it up. Put it on top of the nickel and say some magic words. Then lift away the shaker, still wrapped in the napkin. Everyone will be looking at the coin and thinking you stink as a magician. Quickly drop the salt shaker from the napkin into your lap, but hold the napkin so it looks as if it is still there. Ask if you can try again. With a little drama, say the magic words as you push down on the napkin. Exclaim, "But of course! The nickel has made the salt shaker disappear! I am the greatest magician there ever was!" Cue applause!

SET THE DINNER TABLE AND PUT SOME PRETTY FLOWERS IN THE CENTER

Helping around the house before your parents have to resort to begging, bribing, and/or pleading is always a good call. For this deed, lend a hand at dinnertime and set the table with plates, cutlery, and napkins. Then, for the finishing touch, put a bunch of flowers in a vase of water in the middle of the table. Even one flower will look pretty and make your mom smile.

When dinner is over, tell your mom and dad to relax while you clear away the plates and put everything in the dishwasher or sink. Double deed done!

MAKE GRANDPA HIS FAVORITE TREAT

Your Grandpa makes you happy, right? Grandparents are very good at the happiness thing. So why not make him happy by treating him to something he really likes? Get in the kitchen and whip up a goodie for Grandpa. Who knows? He may just decide to reward you with a very embarrassing story from your mom or dad's childhood. Everybody wins!

LEAVE AN UPLIFTING NOTE ON THE BUS OR SUBWAY

If you travel by bus or subway, you certainly know that sometimes getting from A to B feels more like getting from A to Z. So here's a sneaky way to do a random good deed for someone. Write down something uplifting on a piece of paper or Post-it note®. Leave it behind and maybe you will inspire someone to pass along a positive message of their own. Kindness…pass it on…

TREAT SOMEONE TO A NEW DECK OF CARDS AND SHOW 'EM SOME TRICKS

★ ★

Have you fallen foul of the 52 Pick-up Trick? That's the one when your friend pulls out a deck of cards, and asks you if you'd like to play 52 Pick Up. Then he scatters them on the floor and asks you to pick all 52 cards up. This book is NOT SUGGESTING this as a GOOD DEED. In fact, it's NOT A VERY NICE THING TO DO. Instead, you should pick up a deck of cards next time you are in the drugstore or convenience store, give them to someone as a little gift, and then teach them a couple of card tricks. Don't be a joker—be a good-deed-doer.

TEACH A KID HOW TO THROW A PASS

★ ★

There is nothing like watching a beautifully thrown football pass spiral through the air on a perfect fall day (unless you are more of a basketball, baseball, or soccer kid.) If there is a young football fanatic in your life, you can make his day by giving him a few pointers on his pass. Remind him to hold the ball correctly and work with him on his grip. Show him how to get your arm into the right throwing position and just when to release it to get the most awesome spiral. Talk him through it all and give him plenty of encouragement. This deed is enough to make you a champion (at least, in his eyes). Go get 'em!

SNEAK A NOTE INTO YOUR SISTER'S LUNCH

Yes, there may be times when you've wanted to sneak a spider into your sister's lunch box. But one of the best kinds of good deeds to do is the totally unexpected kind.

So, take a few minutes to think about something your sister does that makes you like her. Go on, there must be something. Is she really good at telling jokes? Are you secretly proud of her for getting such a good grade on that test she was stressing about? Do you think she is probably the most awesome soccer player ever to set foot on the school playing field? Write it down on a piece of paper, and put it in her lunch box. No, do not put it in her sandwich! Remember, good deeds are for sisters, too.

PLAY 20 QUESTIONS TO KEEP YOUR SIBLINGS ENTERTAINED IN THE CAR

Family car trips can be a little bit stressful. The driver needs to concentrate on the road, not smooth the ride for everyone else all the time. You can do a good deed for your mom and dad by keeping everyone out of their hair and entertained in the car. A classic game like I-Spy or 20 Questions will help everyone pass the time as the miles pass along. You don't even need a pencil and paper (but if you have some, you could also try license-plate bingo or hangman). This good deed will help the road trip roll right along.

POP SOME CORN FOR SOMEONE WATCHING A MOVIE

If someone in your house has just settled down on the couch to watch a movie or their very favorite must-see TV show, try this good deed. Sneak into the kitchen, and as quietly as you can, make some popcorn. (OK, we admit it, popping corn can be kind of noisy but try to keep the noise down, especially if the person is watching a silent movie. . .). Put it in a nice big bowl (with some melted butter if that's the way they like it), and deliver it with a smile. You will certainly be POPular.

MAKE A COOKIE KIT

Everyone likes cookies, right? And homemade cookies are the best-ever treats, right? And if those cookies are warm right from the oven (with a cold glass of milk) it just doesn't get any better, right? Make a cookie kit for someone, so that next time they crave freshly baked cookies, they'll have almost everything they need. You'll need some ziplock bags in various sizes, a copy of your favorite cookie recipe, and all the dry ingredients in the recipe. Measure out the ingredients and put each one in a ziplock bag. Then find a suitable container to hold everything, along with a copy of the recipe. You could use a gift bag or box, or a clean glass jar. Decorate it any way you like. You are guaranteed at least a dozen thank-yous for this good deed, and if you are very lucky, you may even get a cookie.

PACK AN EXTRA SANDWICH IN YOUR LUNCH BOX AND SHARE IT WITH SOMEONE

Did you know that sandwiches were named for an 18th-century English nobleman who wanted to have something to eat without having to put his playing cards down, or get them all messy? His title was the Earl of Sandwich, which is a pretty cool one.

So think, then, when you are making a sandwich, of this ye olde guy who loved his snacks as much as he loved his card games. Make a second sandwich in his honor. Pop it in your bag, and when the lunch bell rings, treat someone like a lord and offer them the extra one. It's a noble thing to do!

BE A FRIEND WHEN YOUR FRIEND HAS CHICKEN POX

First, you notice one little red spot and within days your entire body looks as if you've been polka-dotted. Chicken pox is an itchy and irritating illness, so if you've got a friend who's stuck at home with a bad case, be a pal. Don't do anything rash (ha ha) while he's contagious, but send texts and e-mail jokes and call him up to check on him. When he starts to feel better, pay him a visit. Do not ask if you can connect the dots. Bring some homework from school so he doesn't fall behind, and try to cheer him up. He will spot that you are a true buddy.

HELP YOUR SISTER WITH HER HOMEWORK

Show your sister that siblings aren't all bad. Sit down with her after school and offer to help her with her homework. You might use the time to have a little chat with her, too, to make sure everything is OK.

P.S. Easy (unless it's math)

MAKE YOUR BROTHER'S BED

Do you know that in your lifetime, you will spend an average of some 194,000 hours asleep? That is quite a long nap, isn't it? You don't want to spend even one of those hours in a messy bed, though. Make it a habit to make your bed right after you get up every morning. And for a good deed, why not make your brother's bed, too?

P.S. Do not short-sheet the bed, no matter how hard it is to resist the temptation. Otherwise you will have to go back to the start of this book.

LET YOUR PARENTS SLEEP IN ON A SATURDAY

Catching zzzzzzZZZZZZZZZZzzzzs is a good thing to do, but sometimes there are never enough zzzzzzzzZZZZZZZZZzzzzzzzZZZ ZZZZZZZZZs in the nighttime. So it's good to catch a few extra zzzzzZZZZZZZZzzzzs by sleeping in. Do your parents a favor one Saturday morning, and don't wake them up. Fix yourself some breakfast. Make some for your little brother or sister, too. Studies have shown that parents who catch more zzzzZZZZZzzzzs are more relaxxxxxxxxxxed.

COLLECT TOOTHBRUSHES, COMBS, AND PERSONAL CARE ITEMS FOR A HOMELESS SHELTER

Everyone likes a fresh new toothbrush, a bar of soap right out of the wrapper, and a new tube of toothpaste yet to be squeezed. These things may seem like a fairly small deal to you, but someone homeless might really appreciate a gift of new personal care items. Collect donations as a solo or group project and give the gift of a toothbrush…and a smile.

CATCH AND REMOVE A SPIDER FOR SOMEONE

Did you know that there are about 37,000 different species of spiders? You probably know spiders have eight legs that can run up your leg, but did you know they often have eight eyes, too? The better to see you with! There are lots of people who totally freak when they encounter a spider. Even thinking about the 37,000 different kinds makes them shudder. You can do a very good deed for the arachnaphobic person in your life by offering to catch and remove an unwanted spider visitor. Just cover it with a glass, slide a thin piece of cardboard underneath, and tip the whole caboodle over, keeping the cardboard on top of the glass as a lid. Take the spider outside and let him go. **Repeat 36,999 more times!**

PICK UP THE PHONE INSTEAD OF E-MAILING OR TEXTING

You multi-tasker, you! IM'ing your friends while you check texts from another and go through your e-mail inbox. Got to stay connected, right? That's all true, but people (especially parents and family) might like to hear your voice from time to time. So, for this good deed, promise to pick up the phone (cell phones work, too) and call someone up instead of e-mailing or texting. Laugh a little, share a joke, make them smile.

COMPLIMENT YOUR SISTER ON HER VIOLIN PLAYING

The violin is a really tricky instrument for a beginner to learn. When the bow is pulled across one of its strings, you never know what sound might come out. You might get a beautiful, clear musical note, for example, or you might end up with a screeching, tuneless sound that has more in common with an upset cat than music. If your sister is learning to play the violin (or any instrument), be extremely nice to her. Tell her you're proud of her for taking up the challenge, and even if what comes out of her violin is not yet music to your ears (or to anyone's ears, for that matter), let her know that she's getting better all the time. Do not cross your fingers behind your back. This is an easy-to-difficult good deed, depending on your sister's playing.

SAVE THE LAST COOKIE FOR SOMEONE ELSE

No matter how much you think you deserve a cookie, no matter how much you want that cookie, no matter how often and how loud that cookie calls your name, promise you will never, ever eat the last cookie in the cookie jar. There will be somebody who needs to have a cookie just a smidgen more than you do, and they will be very happy to find one there in the jar when they put their hand inside.

SECRETLY FOLD THE LAUNDRY

This is your TOP SECRET GOOD DEED mission, should you choose to accept it. When the clothes dryer cycle finishes, proceed to the laundry stealthily and open the dryer door very carefully. If the items inside are suitably dry, remove them with the utmost caution. Now fold them, matching pairs of socks if necessary, and leave them on the top of the dryer. Run away. Wait for Agent Mom to discover your good deed. You have a license to fold.

SIT NEXT TO SOMEONE WHO IS SITTING ALONE IN CHURCH OR AT THE SYNAGOGUE

People attend religious services to worship together, so if you see someone who is alone, ask them if they mind if you sit down next to them. That's all there is to it!

GIVE A PIGGY-BACK RIDE TO YOUR NIECE OR NEPHEW

Remember how fun it was to get a piggy-back ride? It felt all bumpy and silly and made everyone laugh. Now you are big enough to offer a piggy-back to a little kid in your family. Both of you will get the giggles. It's best to horse around outside in the soft grass, just in case.

TOAST SOME MARSHMALLOWS FOR YOUR LITTLE BROTHER

Mmmmmm…marshmallows are so good in so many ways, but especially toasted to golden, melting perfection over a campfire. It's impossible to eat just one toasted marshmallow. If you've got a little brother (or sister) who is not quite the right age to toast their own treats safely, make sure you toast a few for him (or her). Let them cool down a little bit and serve with a big smile.

If you use the marshmallows to make s'mores, then that is even s'more of a good deed.

DONATE BARELY USED TOYS TO A LOCAL PEDIATRICIAN'S PRACTICE

Waiting around to see the doctor is sometimes boring even for you, so imagine how tough it can be for a little kid who's feeling sick and cranky. They can be the most impatient patients of all, especially if there's nothing to distract them. Why not offer a few second-hand toys that you have grown out of to your doctor's office? The jack-in-the box might not make you smile anymore, but if you pop it over to the doctor's waiting area, it may delight another kid. This good deed is just what the doctor ordered.

SPEND AN ENTIRE DAY BEING A GLASS-HALF-FULL PERSON

Observe this glass of water carefully. From your observations, is the glass A) half-empty, or B) half-full? Your good deed, should you care to accept it, is to spend a whole day following Plan B.

CARRY SOMEONE'S TRAY AT THE FOOD COURT

If you're grabbing a snack at the food court in the local mall and see someone with their hands full, maybe juggling packages, trays, and kids, don't be a court jester. Be a knight of the round (or square) table. Step up and offer to lend a helping hand. Then gallop away on your trusty steed . . . or in your mom's minivan. Whatever.

COLOR SOME EASTER EGGS FOR AN OLDER NEIGHBOR

If decorating Easter eggs is a family tradition in your house, then this year, color a half-dozen or so extra eggs, put them in a pretty Easter basket, and deliver them (with a spring in your step) to an older neigbor. Include a note wishing them a happy holiday. It's a small thing to do, but it is eggs-tra nice.

TEACH SOMEONE HOW TO CLIMB A TREE

Climbing a tree is a classic part of childhood. It's way cool to get up high, admire the view, and look at the neighborhood from a different perspective. Why not share your top tree-climbing tips with someone else, who may not be as confident? Branch out a little. Show her the best kinds of trees to climb, but don't just leaf it there—tell her how to test branches for stability, how to clamber up safely, and most important of all, how to get down again.

FISH OUT ALL THE CHANGE FROM THE BACK OF THE COUCH AND DONATE IT

It may look like a soft and comfy place to sit, but the couch may also double as a piggy bank. Change from people's pockets tends to slide out down the back and sit there behind the sofa cushions. Since people have already donated that money to the couch, why not dig deep, collect all the money lurking there, and donate it to your favorite charity? Sofa, so good!

141

GIVE SOMEONE A HUG

1. E X T E N D   A R M S .
2. WRAP AROUND PERSON.
3. S Q U E E Z E .
4. REPEAT AS NECESSARY.

DONATE A BAG OF GROCERIES TO A NEEDY FAMILY AT THANKSGIVING

You probably have a lot to be thankful for, even if you don't count your sister and you count your pet twice. To help out those who aren't as fortunate, collect canned goods or other grocery items for needy families around the Thanksgiving holiday. You could do this as a class activity. Contact a local house of worship or shelter to offer your donations. They will ensure that the groceries are delivered to a very thankful family.

REMEMBER PEOPLE'S NAMES

Hey, you! No, not you. The one on the left. No, not that far on the left.

Yep, you. Oh, actually, not you. You! What's your name again?

It's not very cool to meet someone and then instantly forget his name, but it does happen. When you meet someone new, try to really glue his name in your head so you can un-glue it and use it again. Think about how you would feel if the sneaker was on the other foot. It is so much nicer to be known by your name, rather than "the kid who does good deeds but has a really super-short memory for names."

PULL THE PLUG ON YOUR CELL-PHONE CHARGER

Are you one of those kids whose cell phone is almost glued to your ear? Well, eventually it runs out of juice, and you have to charge it up. Do a good deed while you are at it, and unplug your charger when the job is done. Sources estimate that only about 5 percent of the power used by cell-phone chargers is actually used to power up the phone. The remaining 95 percent is wasted, by leaving chargers plugged into the wall, but not into phones. Dude! Don't do that.

Pull the plug and love the planet.

When your phone is all charged up, call a friend and ask them to do the same thing.

TAKE A DOG FOR A WALK

What you hear: Woof! Woof! Woooooof! Woof!

What you would hear if you could speak dog: *Come on, kid, take me for a walk! Will ya? Please? Go on, you know it will be fun for both of us. I'll be good, I promise! I won't dig up the neighbor's flower bed like before. I'm a reformed dog.*

What you say: Hey Fido, wanna go for a walk?

What you hear: *Whoo whoo woof! Woof! Woof!*

What you would hear if you could speak dog: *Yes! Whoo whoo! Cool! Thanks, kid. Let's go.*

HAND OUT GOLD STARS

Next time you are in the stationery aisle at the drugstore or discount store, pick up a package of shiny gold stick-on stars. Get in the habit of carrying them around, and when you see someone do a good deed, you can reward them with a gold star. It's a little silly, but something about those stickers makes people happy, and everyone wants to be a star for a day.

GO TO THE POST OFFICE FOR SOMEONE

Everyone has to wait their turn in line sometime right? But for an older person or someone less able to stand than you are, standing in line in the post office can be difficult. Offer to go to the post office (or run some other errand) for someone in this situation, and you have done something pretty outstanding.

GIVE YOUR BEST FRIEND A SINCERE COMPLIMENT

Dear Best Ever Friend,
I know we fight a little bit sometimes...well, actually, we fight a lot, most times. But I wanted you to know that no matter if we do have our differences, I think you are (INSERT A SINCERE COMPLIMENT HERE). I really do, for serious. And no, I'm not up to something. Honest. Really. (Sheesh!)

COLLECT MAGAZINES FOR A DOCTOR'S OR DENTIST'S OFFICE

If you want to catch up on the latest news from two years ago, you might try a doctor's reception area. Sometimes the magazines there are a teeny bit out of date. You can offer to recycle new-ish magazines by donating them to a doctor's or dentist's office. (You could also offer to drop off outdated magazines at the recycling center.)

LET A FRIEND GO FIRST IN A GAME

When you're playing a game with your friend, let him go first. Yes, that's right—even if he always wins and you really really want to go first! Show him that you are just happy to be playing, whether you win or lose, and your thoughtful offer will make him happy and the game all the more enjoyable.

PULL OUT A SHOPPING CART FOR SOMEONE ELSE

Why is it that our hands are often full just when we need them to be empty? If you are at the grocery or discount store, and you see someone juggling car keys, bags, kids, and cell phone while trying to free up a hand to grab a shopping cart, pull one out and roll it over with a smile. It's a small kindness that people really appreciate. And keep the cart with the wobbly wheels for yourself.

HELP HANG OUT THE LAUNDRY

Has your family decided to go green and not use the clothes dryer so often? After all, there is plenty of free, clean sunshine available to dry clothes and make them smell good. Grab a bucket of clothespins and offer to hang up a load of laundry. It's a good thing to do for Mother Earth and your regular mom on Earth. Bring in the clothes when they are dry, and you've done another good deed.

P.S. Do not hang underwear in a highly conspicuous place.

SET UP A WEBCAM FOR SOMEONE

If you have a family friend who has family members living away from home, you could ask them if they'd like you to set up a webcam so they can stay in touch. Share all those computer skills you have learned to help a family stick together. Seeing and speaking with relatives on the webcam is the next best thing to being there. (And there is much less risk of your aunt pinching your cheeks and telling you how much you've grown.)

BUY A SONG FOR A FRIEND

Serenading someone outside her window is very old school. If you want to send a musical message to someone, buy her a song. Most MP3 sites are set up so that you can purchase a download and send it as a gift. Pick a song that suits the moment. If your friend is stressing out about a big test, send an inspiring tune. Send a song that will cheer her up if she's facing some tough times, or a song that will remind her of a fun time with you.

CARRY A COUPLE OF EXTRA BOTTLES OF WATER IN HOT WEATHER

Did you know that our body weight is about 65 percent water? You can see why it's so important to keep hydrated, especially when summer temperatures sizzle. You are probably already in the habit of keeping a bottle or container of water with you when you are running around in the summer. Why not throw an extra bottle or two in your backpack, to give to someone who's looking thirsty? Then, drink in their appreciation for a deed well done.

CLEAN OUT YOUR CLOSET AND DONATE TO CHARITY

There is probably stuff in the back of your closet or cabinet that hasn't seen the light of day for some time. Outgrown, unloved, and unwanted clothes and shoes in good condition can be donated to a thrift store or put in special clothing recycling boxes. So clean out your closet, recycle, and award yourself a good deed.

HELP A PARENT CARRY A STROLLER UP THE STAIRS

When you are out and about, you are probably already looking for opportunities to do good deeds, right? That's what got you so far along in this book! If you see someone struggling with a stroller on a stairway, for example, get in there and lend a hand. Way to go, kid.

LEARN THE NAMES OF PEOPLE WHO WORK AT THE CORNER STORE

There are probably lots of people in your life you know by sight, but not by name. Try finding out the names of some of these people so you can use them when you greet them. If you are a regular customer at the corner store, for example, it's great to say, "Hi, Jim!" or "What's up, Sandra?" (But not if their names are Tom and Betty!) Share your name, too. It's a tiny good deed that makes the whole wide world seem like a smaller, friendlier place.

HELP SOMEONE PICK UP THEIR SCHOOL BOOKS

It is embarrassing enough when your school books slip out of your arms and papers and books spill all over a busy hallway. Having to pick everything up again can add to the blush-inducing feeling. If you come across someone scrabbling around for their books and bits and pieces, stop and help. Your smile and your kindness will go a long way toward easing the embarrassment they are feeling.

THANK YOUR SPORTS COACH FOR BEING AN INSPIRATION

They're the people who are always behind you, urging you to be your best. A great coach can help inspire you to reach the top of your game, whatever that game may be. You do thank the coach every time you play, but this time, let words speak louder than actions, and tell your coach what a fantastic inspiration he or she really is. Everyone wins!

GIVE A BIG (BUT QUIET) THANK YOU TO A LIBRARIAN

Keeping your voice down, let your librarian know that she's tops in your books. Raise your admiration level but not the level of your voice. Let your warm thoughts speak volumes.

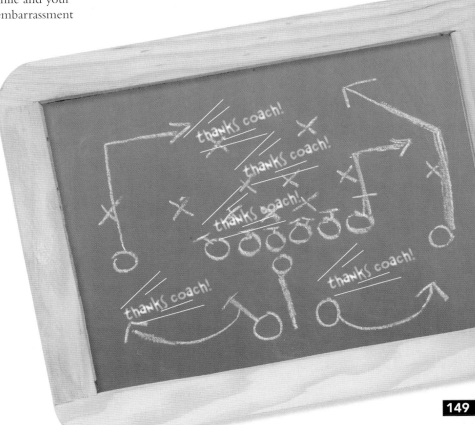

"Change will no
wait for some ot
some other tim
ones we've been
are the change

t come if we
her person or
e. We are the
waiting for. We
that we seek."

Barack Obama

OFFER TO BABYSIT FOR FREE

Do you know anyone with a baby or young child by any chance who looks a bit tired? Taking care of kids can be exhausting.

Why not volunteer to babysit for a couple of hours. They'll get a much-needed break, you'll have some fun, and doing it for free will qualify as a pretty good deed.

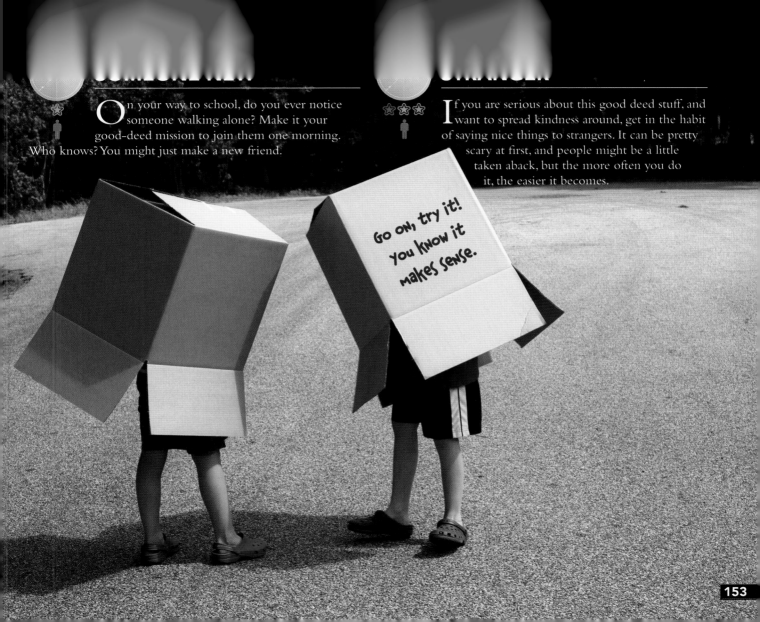

On your way to school, do you ever notice someone walking alone? Make it your good-deed mission to join them one morning. Who knows? You might just make a new friend.

If you are serious about this good deed stuff, and want to spread kindness around, get in the habit of saying nice things to strangers. It can be pretty scary at first, and people might be a little taken aback, but the more often you do it, the easier it becomes.

Go on, try it! You know it makes sense.

MAKE HOLIDAY COOKIES AND DELIVER THEM TO A SHELTER

Holiday cookie-baking is a big tradition for many families. Start a new tradition this year by promising to donate a tray of decorated cookies to the local shelter. It's a great idea to get a group of people together, friends or family, to have a cookie-baking day. Everyone can make their favorites, then you can divide them up at the end of the day so each person gets a variety of yummy treats. Wrap up a tray for the shelter and deliver it together. Promise to do the same next year.

SET UP APPRECIATION DAYS FOR SCHOOL EMPLOYEES

Everyone likes to feel that they are doing a good job, yet if you went around to everyone at school to tell them what great work they are doing, you would be very, very late for class.

Instead, speak with your class teacher or principal about setting up a regular staff appreciation day to thank the non-teachers who work at your school, from cafeteria workers to janitors. A thank you is a very welcome thing.

CATCH SOMEONE BEING KIND

Pssssst! If you catch someone red-handed in the act of being kind, let them know that

their good deed has not gone unnoticed. Make eye contact and smile, and remember that kindness is contagious.

SET UP A PET PLAY DATE

Having a pet is a big responsibility, but it's also lots of fun. Set aside a certain part of every day to play with your pet. Play catch with the dog, give the cat a brush, give your hamster a spin in his ball, or admire your fish as they swim. It's not only good for your pet, scientists think it's good for you, too, as petting an animal or watching fish in an aquarium are both thought to reduce stress. You might get licked on the nose, too! Although we wouldn't expect this from a fish.

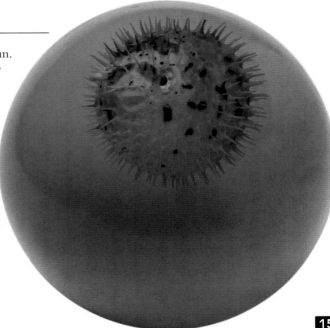

WAVE HELLO TO EVERYONE TODAY

Today, you are going to be a one-kid wave machine! Get out there and greet people with a wave, a smile, and a cheerful "Hi." Will your arm hurt by the end of the day? Will your smiling muscles ache? We hope so. That's the idea.

TEXT SOMEONE WHO IS HAVING A BAD DAY

If your friend is going through a rough day, you may not be able to roll back the sunrise and start it all over again. It's also not always possible to make everything better. They may not even be ready to talk about it yet. So, do a good deed and send them a text. Let them know that you are there when they're ready.

TEACH A KID TO TIE HIS SHOELACES

Do you remember how great it was finally to be able to tie your own shoelaces? It's a little thing to learn, but one big step on the way to becoming a big kid. Sit down with a little kid and help them follow in your footsteps. Show them how to tie up their shoes. They will knot forget the nice kid who helped them, and wouldn't shoe like to be that kid?

PUT A BIRTHDAY IN A BOX

I f you can't be together with someone you care about on their special day, send them a birthday box. Make it just as unique and individual as your friend or relative. After all, anyone can send a present or a card, but not everyone can send an entire birthday! Here's what to do:

- At a party store, get a few inexpensive birthday decorations: balloons, streamers, confetti, noisemakers, party hats, candy, and small party favors.

- Buy a snack-sized cake or individually-wrapped brownie (something suitable for mailing), and a birthday candle.

- Put everything in a small box, protecting the contents with bubble wrap. Mail it in plenty of time for his or her big day! You'll get a line of thank-yous, each one bigger than the last.

WRITE A THANK-YOU NOTE TO YOUR MAIL CARRIER

The walls of a post office in New York City are inscribed with this saying: "Neither snow nor rain nor heat nor gloom of night stays these couriers from the swift completion of their appointed rounds." Maybe there is no mention of dog bites, but you have to admit, our mail carriers do an awesome job. Let them know that we appreciate them in a way that only they can truly appreciate: write them a thank-you letter!

START A CONVERSATION WITH SOMEONE YOU DON'T KNOW AT SCHOOL

If you go to a big school, there are probably lots of kids there you don't know. Even in a small school there might be a few unknown people. Don't let anyone be a stranger. Find someone you don't know, and start up a conversation. This is kind of tricky, but hang in there. Talk a little, and listen up, too. You'll have this to say for yourself: you've done yet another good deed.

PAT SOMEONE ON THE BACK

This one's easy: pat someone deserving on the back (they don't have to be named Pat) and tell them they've done good. Done.

PICK UP TRASH, EVEN IF IT ISN'T YOURS

There are lots of careless litterbugs out there who are happy to drop trash wherever they like, as long as it's not in the trash can. Don't let the litterbugs bug you too much. Instead, if you see trash, pick it up, even if it isn't yours, and dispose of it properly.

ASK GRANDMA FOR HER FAVORITE RECIPE

Does your Grandma make the best apple pie in the known (or unknown) universe? Or, is there another dish that she's great at cooking? Even if the best thing Grandma makes for dinner is reservations, there must be something she cooks that knocks your socks off. Ask her to write the recipe down for you, and keep it in a safe place.

SEND A CARD TO A LONG-LOST RELATIVE

Does your family tree have more branches than you can keep track of? If you've lost touch with a relative, why not drop them a quick note (a postcard is perfect) just to say hello? You could even send them Grandma's recipe if she doesn't mind. Don't wait until holiday time, just send it whenever you think of it. We'll go out on a limb here: you might make someone's day!

Grandma's apple pie recipe

GRANDMA'S RECIPE

ADDRESS

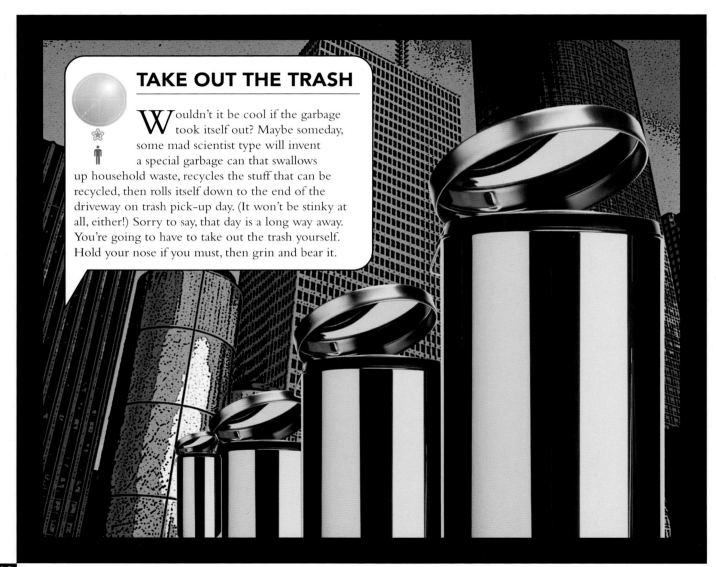

TAKE OUT THE TRASH

Wouldn't it be cool if the garbage took itself out? Maybe someday, some mad scientist type will invent a special garbage can that swallows up household waste, recycles the stuff that can be recycled, then rolls itself down to the end of the driveway on trash pick-up day. (It won't be stinky at all, either!) Sorry to say, that day is a long way away. You're going to have to take out the trash yourself. Hold your nose if you must, then grin and bear it.

ADDRESS

FLOWERS

DO UNTO OTHERS CERTIFICATE

THIS CERTIFICATE ENTITLES THE BEARER TO ONE GOOD DEED OF HIS OR HER OWN CHOOSING. YOU MAY REDEEM AT ANY TIME; THERE IS NO EXPIRATION DATE. PLEASE CONTACT _____ TO REDEEM YOUR GOOD DEED. IT IS APPROPRIATE TO ACKNOWLEDGE THE COMPLETION OF THE DEED WITH A THANK-YOU AND A SMILE. THIS CERTIFICATE IS FOR THE SOLE USE OF THE BEARER AND MAY NOT BE TRANSFERRED, SOLD, OR EXCHANGED FOR CHOCOLATE.

INTRODUCE YOURSELF

"Hello, my name is _____!"

Chances are there is someone you see every day who doesn't know your name. You might be on smiling or nodding terms, you may have even exchanged words, but that person doesn't know you from Adam. (If your name is Adam, this expression won't work. Please ignore and read on.) Seize the day today, walk up to that person and say, "Hello, you!"

"My name is _____. I am pleased to meet you."

GIVE YOUR HOMEROOM TEACHER BREAKFAST

Your teacher is always telling you that students learn better if they start each day with a good breakfast. Wonder if they take their own advice? Wonder no more! One morning, get to class early with a mug of takeout coffee and a pastry. Add a piece of fruit...apples are the obvious ones, but you might feel like going bananas. Who knows? Teachers may start coming to class in their jammies.

ASK SOMEONE IF THEY NEED HELP

Life isn't a bowl of cherries, they say, and there are plenty of times when we all need a helping hand, whether it's someone to steady a stepladder when you are changing a light bulb, open the door when your arms are full, or help you figure out how to buy a train ticket. Pretend you are a Good Deed Superhero and whenever you see someone struggling or looking a little out of their depth, try the Magic Five Little Words: Hey, do you need help?

P.S. A cape is optional.

GIVE SOMEONE AN ANONYMOUS PRESENT

Next time you are browsing in the discount store, pick out one or two small but useful things. This could be anything from a new pack of gum to a novelty pen. Tie a ribbon around each gift, and leave it in a public place for someone to find.

CALL OR VISIT A PERSON WHO IS STUCK AT HOME

If you know someone who is unable to leave home for one reason or another, he or she may get pretty bored by their own four walls. Do a good deed and pay them a visit. Stopping by for even a quick chat can lift both your spirits. If you can't visit in person, call up or send an e-mail.

GIVE SOMEONE YOUR UNDIVIDED ATTENTION

One of the nicest, most flattering gifts you can give to someone is the gift of your attention. When someone is talking to you, make eye contact and smile. Listen to them as if they were the only person on Earth. Do not divide your attention; multiply it.

RAKE UP LEAVES

Fall leaves are certainly beautiful when they are dappled in sunshine and moving in the breeze. But when they are soggy and piled up high in the yard, they are a little less great, you must admit. Do a favor for a neighbor who is less able than you to do yardwork. Show up one day with a rake and move those leaves into smaller, easy-to-handle piles. Then you can bag them up and take the bags to the curb ready for pick-up, or you can compost them. You won't be-leaf how grateful this deed will make someone.

FOR SOMEONE

TREAT A SPECIAL KID TO A NEW BOX OF CRAYONS AND A COLORING BOOK

New crayons are possibly one of the best things in the world, no matter how old you are. They look so pretty lined up in their neat rows, they smell waxy and nice, and they really do promise hours of fun. A new coloring book is a real treat, too. The owner will be able to pick the very best picture in the book and color that one in first. Next time you are in the discount store or drugstore, pick up a box of crayons and select a fun-looking coloring book for a special kid you know. It won't break the bank but it will make someone happy.

P.S. Why not offer to do some coloring with him or her? It's probably something you've grown out of, but it actually is relaxing.

TREAT YOUR DAD LIKE IT'S FATHER'S DAY ON A DAY THAT ISN'T

Here's how to really confuse your dad: pick a day, and all day long treat him just like it's Father's Day. Bring him the morning paper or breakfast in bed. Make sure he gets to be in charge of the television remote. Bring him a soft drink and fluff up the couch cushions before he sits down. Don't pick fights with your brother. You certainly will get him thinking. He may even think you are trying to get a raise in your allowance by being so good. He may just give it to you. Now that's payback.

TIDY UP THE HALLWAY

When you open the door and step inside your house or apartment, what does the hallway say to you? Does it say, "Hi, welcome to our neat and tidy home!" Or, does it say, "Help! We've been ransacked! Oh, no, we're just messy." Or, does it not say anything at all, because it is a hallway? You can ponder that thought as you complete this good deed: giving your hallway a good clean-up. Bring a trash bag and cleaning supplies like a dustpan and broom, cloths, and cleaning spray. Pick up anything that lives somewhere else and put it away. Pare down the coat racks.

Do you really need three different jackets hanging there, or can a couple go back in your closet? Same goes with shoes and backpacks. Lift stuff on the floor up and sweep out any dust. Throw any trash stuff into the bag as you go. Use the cloth to dust any hall furniture down (with cleaning spray, if appropriate). There! A tidy hallway at last.

WHEN THE FIRST STRAWBERRIES ARRIVE, BUY A BOX FOR YOUR MOM

Delicious, yummy, squishy, fruity strawberries. Mmmmm. When the first local strawberries of the season arrive at the farmer's market or supermarket, pick the best-looking box and buy it for your mom. While it is true that a box of strawberries is not exactly a bouquet of roses, they will be appreciated just as much. (And maybe she will share them!)

PUT A NOTE IN YOUR MOM'S PURSE OR BRIEFCASE

Moms are really busy people. They are often so busy running around all over the place that they barely have time to stop. So, imagine that when they do stop, and fish around in their briefcase for a magazine to read or dig through their purse to find some chewing gum, what they find is a very nice note from you. That would be a very nice thing, wouldn't it? It's never a bad thing to make your mom smile.

TAPE A COUPLE OF QUARTERS TO A PAY PHONE

These days it seems like everyone and his dog has a cell phone (cats do not seem to use cell phones.) But even now, there are times when someone might need to make a call but can't. Maybe they've run out of power or can't get a signal. Imagine that they go to a pay phone and find they don't have any change. Suddenly, they spot enough money for a call taped to the side of the phone. That is going to feel like a pretty amazing surprise, isn't it? For this good deed, tape a couple of quarters to the phone with some masking tape.

You can even draw on a smiley face.

SPEND THE DAY WITH YOUR GRANDPARENTS

The U.S. Census Bureau says there about 56 million grandparents in the United States today, but NONE of them is just like yours. Grandparents are wonderful. Whether you have one grandparent or the complete set of four, set aside a special day to spend with them. Bring along your siblings if you want to have a real multigenerational extravaganza. Plan something really fun. Here are some suggestions for things to do:

13. Have breakfast in a diner ✓

14. Set up the karaoke machine and get singing

15. Go canoeing or kayaking

16. Visit a local museum or attraction and be a tourist in your own town

17. Go on the swings in the playground

18. Do watercolor portraits of each other (or fingerpaints for little kids)

19. Play board games

20. Go to a pick-your-own farm and load up on berries

21. Take a nature hike

22. Get language CDs from the library and learn another language together

23. Play miniature golf or go bowling

1. Go fly a kite ✓

2. Hit the movies

3. Drive to somewhere special from the past (the house your grandparents grew up in, your first school, etc.)

4. Find an old-fashioned ice-cream stand and order a cone

5. Go on a picnic at your local park (or even in your own backyard)

6.

7.

8.

9.

10.

LEARN TO SAY HELLO IN ANOTHER LANGUAGE

As well as learning to say "Hi" in 36 different languages, you'll have to do a bit of research if you can't identify all the countries represented below. Learning that is a global good deed, indeed.

 Tung

 Al salaam a'alaykum

 Dumella rah

 Sok sabai jie te

 Ni hao

 Nazdar

 Päivää

 Bonjour

 Guten Tag

 Yassou

 Shalom

 Szia

 Namaste

 Selamat pagi

 Dia dhuit

 Buongiorno

 Konnichiwa

 Kia ora

 God dag

 Czesc

 Bom dia

 Sat sri akal

 Zdravstvuite

 Dobar dan

 Živijo

 Hola

 Jambo

 God Dag

 Ii ho bo

 Sa-wa dee krap

 Tashi delek

Merhaba

Annyong hashimnikka

 Bore da

 Salam

 Bom dia

GIVE SOMEONE DIRECTIONS IF THEY LOOK LOST

No doubt you know your neighborhood like the back of your hand, but if you come across someone with a map in his hands and an extremely puzzled expression on his face, don't tell him to get lost, because chances are, he already is. Please stop and ask if you can help him with some handy directions. This kind of helping hand to a stranger is a fantastic good deed, and a real step in the right direction to finishing all the good deeds in this book.

ADOPT A HIGHWAY, BEACH, OR PARK

Congratulations! You are the proud parent of a bouncing baby beach. OK, not really. But you can take care of your world and do a good deed for your entire community by choosing to adopt a stretch of street, beach, or park for a year. This is a perfect activity for a group, as you'll need plenty of helping hands. Celebrate your adoption with a big clean-up day. Throughout the year, hold regular days to collect and remove trash and recycle stuff that can be recycled. Contact your local parks department to find out if there is a volunteer program in place already. Some offer special training in return for your generously donated time.

CUT OUT A FUNNY COMIC AND TAPE IT TO SOMEONE'S LOCKER

Making someone smile is always a very good deed to do. One cool way to achieve it is to recycle a comic from a book or newspaper. Pick one that's made you giggle in the past. Cut it out and then use a little tape to stick it to a friend's locker at school. Laughter, like kindness, is contagious.

"Never look anybody unl helping him

down on

ess you're

up."

Jesse Jackson

Watermelon must be the most delicious summertime treat. It's just made for eating outside, not just because it can get a little bit sloppy, but also because you can hold excellent seed-spitting contests with your friends. Chill a watermelon in the fridge until it's nice and cool, ask a parent to help to cut it into slices, and serve it up to your neighbors and friends. Life is sweet.

PUT IN A POWER STRIP

You know that computers, televisions, and DVD players on standby look as if they are doing nothing, but are actually gobbling up energy when no one is looking, don't you? We figured you did. Still, it can be a little annoying going all through the house every night shutting off switches, especially if you have fallen asleep in front of the TV. So here's what to do: go to the hardware or discount store and purchase a power strip. Then, plug all the energy-gobblers into it. Voila! Now there is only one switch to hit to save energy. What a bright idea…and a good deed.

OFFER TO RETURN LIBRARY BOOKS FOR A FRIEND OR NEIGHBOR

The library is a fine place, but if people don't bring books back on time, they will find themselves facing a fine. Little fines can build up over time until they reach an amount that is not really fine at all—plus, there might be a fine person who is just waiting to read the book. Offer to do this fine deed for a friend or neighbor.

PLAY FRISBEE WITH A DOG

We all know that dogs love to chase this and that—well, just about anything in fact. You love to throw Frisbees. Think about it, what else is there to say? Deed done!

TAKE A CPR CLASS

FYI: "CPR" stands for "cardiopulmonary resuscitation." Can you say that three times fast? Even if it's a difficult thing to pronounce, it's a very important thing to know, because with CPR training, you can learn how to save a life. As good deeds go, that probably tops the charts. So, sign up and learn how to do CPR. ASAP. OK?

VOLUNTEER AS A KID'S COACH

Go on, kid! You can do it! I'm right behind you, cheering you on. Share your love of sports and the thrills, spills, and challenges of competing by volunteering to coach a kid's team. Check with your local YMCA, parks and recreation department, or kid's club for opportunities. Be inspiring, be encouraging, and above all, show everyone how fun it is to have fun.

WATER A TREE

Trees get thirsty, too, especially in hot weather. Treat your favorite tree to a delicious cool bucket of water once in a while. You can hug the trunk, too, if no one is looking. It's a tree-mendously nice thing to do.

OFFER AN ICE-COLD DRINK TO THE MAIL OR PAPER DELIVERY PERSON ON A HOT DAY

Do you know those days when it's so hot that you could practically fry an egg on the sidewalk? (Although chances are, if you opened the fridge to get an egg, and felt that cool blast of air, you'd never move. And who would want to eat an egg fried on the sidewalk, anyway?) When temperatures soar, spare a thought for the postal worker or paper delivery kid on their daily rounds. Offer him or her an ice-cold drink straight from the depths of the fridge (don't climb in). Then you can drink in the appreciation. It may be hot, but you are cool.

SPEND AN ENTIRE DAY NOT FIGHTING WITH YOUR BROTHER OR SISTER

Sometimes brothers and sisters go together like hot dogs and mustard. Perfect! Sometimes they go together like hot dogs and chocolate syrup. Not so perfect! Do a good deed for your parents (and your whole family) and promise that you will last an entire day, from breakfast time through to bedtime, and beyond, without fighting. That means absolutely none of the following: no scraps, scuffles, fisticuffs, feuds, tussles, brawls, rumbles, squabbles, quarrels, run-ins, tiffs, or spats. For a whole, entire day, got it?

HELP SOMEONE CROSS THE STREET

A little thing like crossing the street can be a big deal for some people. To a little kid, someone loaded down with shopping bags, or someone who's not as mobile as you are, getting from one side of the road to the other can be tricky…even scary sometimes. If you see someone who obviously needs a hand, make sure that hand is yours. You can hold hands with a little kid, carry packages or shopping bags for someone, or extend an arm for a less able person. This good deed is a courteous act that is always appreciated.

BECOME A RECYCLING

LOOK! UP IN THE SKY! IS IT A BIRD? IS IT A PLANE? NO, IT'S RECYCLING KID!

FASTER THAN A SPEEDING BULLET AT SEPARATING OUT ALUMINUM CANS FROM STEEL!

MORE POWERFUL THAN THE URGE TO PUT AN OLD ENVELOPE IN THE TRASH INSTEAD OF THE RECYCLING BOX!

ABLE TO LEAP MOUNTAINS OF BUNDLED NEWSPAPER IN A SINGLE BOUND!

Use your head: it makes sense to use things again, doesn't it? Recycling rules. It can save energy, it helps conserve our natural resources, it can cut pollution, and it stops our landfills filling up. Become a recycling superhero in your home, at school, and in the community. Teach yourself about all the reasons we should recycle, and find out every which way we can do it. Make it your goal to recycle as much as you possibly can, leaps and bounds ahead of the crowd. You can also use your super skills to educate reluctant recyclers.

SUPERHERO

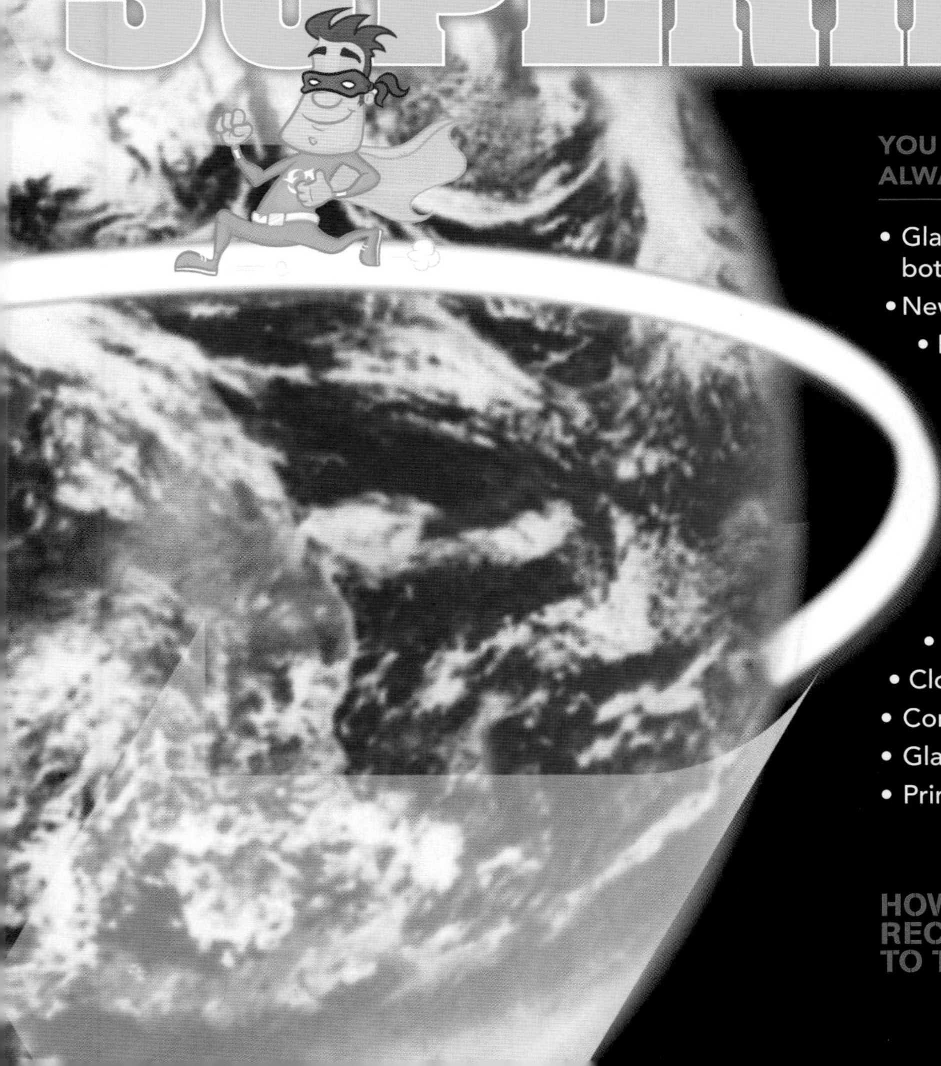

YOU KNOW THAT THIS STUFF SHOULD ALWAYS BE RECYCLED:

- Glass jars and bottles
- Newspapers
- Boxes
- Egg cartons
- Magazines
- White paper
- All aluminum (pie pans, foil, cans, etc.)
- Tin cans
- Most plastics

THIS STUFF CAN BE RECYCLED, TOO. ASK YOUR TOWN OR CITY GOVERNMENT ABOUT:

- Batteries
- Clothing
- Computers
- Glasses
- Printer cartridges
- Cell phones
- Paint and decorating materials
- Building materials

HOW MANY MORE SUPER-RECYCLABLES CAN YOU ADD TO THE LIST?

MAKE A BIRDBATH AND BIRD FEEDER

Do a good deed for a feathered friend by making a bird feeder. In winter, it's not always easy for birds to find food, so make sure they can find some at your place. And because it's nice to wash your claws before meals, you could also construct a simple birdbath from old terra–cotta plant pots. The happy birds will sing their thanks to you, all year round.

What you need for the feeder: Empty plastic milk carton (a gallon is best; a sharp knife and your parents' permission to use it; string to hang the feeder.

How to make it: Start with a totally dry carton. With the knife, carefully cut a large opening in the side of the carton, about halfway up. Make the opening big enough so that birds can perch on the edge as they nibble, and so that it is easy for you to fill with seed. Then hang it up outside from a tree or fence, fill with birdseed, and enjoy.

What you need for the birdbath: three terra-cotta plant pots (12 inches, 14 inches, and 16 inches—recycling old ones is fine!); one 20-inch-diameter clay saucer (a glazed, waterproof one is best); strong adhesive; paints to decorate, if desired.

How to make it: First, you need to glue the smallest pot to the saucer. Turn the saucer upside down. Put strong adhesive on the bottom of the flowerpot, and place it in the center of the saucer bottom. Let them dry completely. Then, when you have chosen a site for the birdbath with your parents, put the largest pot upside down, stack with the next largest pot, and top with the smallest pot and saucer. (Always hold those together, even though they are glued.) Admire your work.

P.S. You don't need a soap dish and a stack of little towels.

REMEMBER SOMEONE'S BIRTHDAY

Happy birthday to you, Happy birthday to you Happy birthday dear _____ Happy birthday to you!

P.S. Put all your friends' birthdays on your computer calendar or in a notebook so you never miss a single one!

GIVE MONEY TO CHARITY

Because you are a kid, you probably don't have an enormous income to fund your lavish lifestyle. But no matter how much money you have or don't have, it is a very good deed to donate some of it to the charity of your choice. Even a handful of change can bring about change. So dig deep, and donate.

LEARN TO SAY "HELLO" IN SIGN LANGUAGE

TURN OFF YOUR COMPUTER AND TALK WITH SOMEONE

Yes, your computer is your friend, but there is a whole wide world out there, too. Remember it? Grass, trees, houses, people? While the Internet is a wonderful virtual place, don't forget the real world. For this good deed, shut down your computer, and go find someone to talk to. Hang out, maybe shoot some hoops, or go on a bike ride.

MIND YOUR MANNERS

Manners! Who needs them? Actually, we all do. One of the most important good deeds you can do today (and every day) is to treat people with respect, and practicing good manners is an excellent way to show respect for others. Just in case you were born in a barn, here are the basics:

TREAT OTHERS THE WAY YOU WOULD LIKE TO BE TREATED

GREET PEOPLE APPROPRIATELY

THINK BEFORE YOU SPEAK

DON'T TALK AND CHEW AT THE SAME TIME

SAY "PLEASE" AND "THANK YOU"

DON'T INTERRUPT

LEARN HOW TO INTRODUCE PEOPLE TO EACH OTHER

RESPECT OLDER PEOPLE

DON'T PUT PEOPLE DOWN

FOLLOW THE RULES

SHARE YOUR UMBRELLA
ON A RAINY DAY

When raindrops keep falling on your head, and you've got an umbrella, offer to share it with a friend. That way, both of you can look for rainbows.

COLLECT TRASH AT SCHOOL

A+

Do you want to go to the head of the class without studying or doing any homework? CAN SUCH A THING BE POSSIBLE? Well, sort of ....Talk with the principal about a clean-up day. Suggest that in the last class period of the chosen clean-up day, everybody gets to work picking up trash, collecting recycling, restoring the cafeteria to its former glory, and more? If everyone pitches in, it won't take long to get your school looking smart. (And you will go to the head of the class for making it happen.)

LEAVE A CANDY BAR IN THE VENDING MACHINE

Next time you see a vending machine, go ahead and buy a sweet treat…but leave it in the machine. Oh, yes. The next person who buys something will find a delicious unexpected bonus in the form of a candy bar, pack of gum, or roll of mints. This random act of sweetness will be greatly appreciated.

OPEN A CAR DOOR FOR SOMEONE

If you see someone with an armful of shopping bags or a squirmy baby trying to juggle everything so she can open the car door, say, "Excuse me, can I open that door for you?"

(Oh, yeah, then open the door.)

WRITE A THANK-YOU NOTE TO YOUR PARENTS

Dear Mom and Dad,

I know it's not Mother's Day or Father's Day. It's actually Tuesday. Anyway, I just wanted to take a minute or two to let you know that I am really grateful for all the stuff that you do for me. I might not always act like I appreciate it (although I hope I usually do) but I really, really do.

Here are three examples of cool things you did for me recently:

1)

2)

3)

There are lots more where those came from. I am one lucky kid to have parents like you.

P.S. I promise I am not asking for a bigger allowance.

With a big hug,

your Little Treasure

TEACH SOMEONE SOMETHING YOU KNOW

Everybody's got a hidden talent, whether it's folding the best paper airplanes in the whole world or figuring out where to stand on the subway platform for the best chance of getting a seat. What's your special talent? Teach someone something you're good at, and ask them to teach you something back. You'll both have a new trick up your sleeves, and if you do this with a lot of friends, you'll need some extra sleeves…

PUT YOUR DIRTY SOCKS IN THE LAUNDRY BASKET

Are you under the impression that your socks walk themselves to the laundry basket at the end of the day? You must also think that your shoes line themselves up at the bottom of the closet. It may surprise you to know this, but dirty socks must be placed in the laundry basket (not tossed just short of the basket, please), and shoes are unable to put themselves away. You learn something new every day, don't you?

VOLUNTEER AT THE LOCAL SOUP KITCHEN

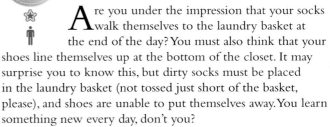

A nice warm meal gives us a warm feeling inside. You can also get a warm feeling inside by volunteering your time at the local soup kitchen. This is an excellent group activity as plenty of helping hands are needed every day. Are you warming to the idea?

MAKE DINNER
FOR THE
WHOLE
FAMILY

Bubbling cauldrons…machines that go ping…all manner of mysterious ingredients in glass jars… does this sound like Dr. Frankenstein's laboratory, or your own kitchen? The answer is, both! In fact, you can think of the kitchen as a science laboratory waiting to be explored. There is actually a lot of science happening when you cook—and you get to eat your experiments, which is pretty cool. So, one evening, steal down to the lab (perhaps with a trusty assistant) and whip up your most spectacular experiment ever: dinner for your whole family. Here's what to do. Pick an evening when everyone's home. Let Mom in on it, so she doesn't make other plans. Set a budget for the meal, and when she gives you the go-ahead, then go ahead.

Plan your menu with care. Look online or browse cookbooks for inspiration. Pick something you think everyone will like, but consider including something new, like a side dish or dessert. Avoid super-complex stuff unless you are an experienced cook. You might want to choose a themed menu, such as Make-Your-Own Chinese Takeout Night or South of the Border Mexican Fiesta Evening. Don't pick Family Food Poisoning Night.

Draw up a shopping list of ingredients. Most of the things you need might already be lurking in the cabinets, so take a good look around. Shop for the other stuff you need, and stick to your budget.

On the big evening, get started early. Go through the recipes and make a simple timetable for what needs doing, when. Keep an eye on the clock to make sure you are on schedule.

Decide if you are going to ask your trusty assistant to do anything, like set the table or handle the beverages. Reward him (or her) handsomely with praise and an extra-large portion of dessert.

Professional chefs lay out everything they are going to need before they begin, so you might want to try that approach. It's also useful to clean up spills and other messes as you go, so the kitchen lab isn't turned into a disaster zone.

GET COOKING!

When dinner is served, summon everyone to your laboratory to experience an experiment in delicious-ness. And don't be a monster...when everyone is finished, put the dishes in the dishwasher and make sure the kitchen looks like it did before you started.

GOOD DEEDS I HAVE DONE

Date

Deed

Notes

Date

Deed

Notes

Date

Deed

Notes

Date

Deed

Notes

Date

Deed

Notes

Date

Deed

Notes

Date

Deed

Notes

Date

Deed

Notes

Acknowledgments

The publisher would like to thanks the following for their kind permission to reproduce their photographs:
(Key: a-above; b-below/bottom; c-center; f-far; l-left; r-right; t-top)

Alamy Images: NASA / Index Stock 147c. Dorling Kindersley: The American Museum of Natural History 19tr; The British Museum 27br; Malcolm Coulson 120l; Emma Firth 66bc; Judith Miller Archive / Cooper Owen 52tr; Judith Miller Archive / Tennants 93; NASA 7br, 180-181; Rough Guides 59b, 116, 125; The Science Museum, London 131cl; Stephen Oliver 44l (12 x bananas), 61ca (egg), 144bc (star); Lindsey Stock 61ftr (green parcel), 61tc (white parcel), 78ca (frame); Barrie Watts 108-109 (trees); Paul Wilkinson 135b. fotolia: Geo Martinez 110cl. iStockphoto.com: Dino Ablakovic 35br; Christine Balderas 40cla, 163br; Selahattin Bayram 4c, 4cl, 4cr, 5c, 5cl, 5cr, 5tc, 5tl, 5tr; Beans- 89 (curtains); Blackred 178; Leon Bonaventura 101; Denice Breaux 184br; David Cannings-Bushell 21b; Ferenc Cegledi 163 (certificate); Sharon Dominick 121bl; Rui Frias 143; Maria Gritcai 176; id-work 83c, 83cr, 83tc, 83tr; Javarman3 4 (background), 5 (background), 6 (background), 7 (background); Matt Jeacock 57; Andrew Johnson 30 (grass), 31 (grass), 118-119; Carl Keyes 140-141; Sven Klaschik 104-105; Matt Knannlein 9 (paper), 10 (paper), 11 (paper), 12 (paper), 13 (paper), 14 (paper), 113br, 187; Kronick 22r; Valerie Loiseleux 163 (border); Alex Mathers 82bl; Zoran Milic 181tl; Vasko Miokovic 117; Dzianis Miraniuk 168bc, 168bl, 168tc, 168tl, 168-169b, 168-169t, 169bc, 169br, 169tc, 169tr; Moodville 186; Pamela Moore 153; Michal Mrozek 146; Andrew Parfenov 6c, 9 (border), 10 (border), 11 (border), 12 (border), 13 (border), 14 (border), 63, 190 (border), 191 (border); Jonathan Parry 16c, 16cr, 16fcr; Lee Pettet 76r; Andrejs Pidjass 188-189; Jim Pruitt 41 (certificate); Alejandro Raymond 62; Amanda Rohde 102bl; Ray Roper 127br; Anssi Ruuska 18; Jon Schulte 149cr (chalk play); Alexander Sienkiewicz 95bl; Mark Stay 172; James Steidl 152; Willie B. Thomas 97; Emrah Turudu 129; Boris Zaytsev 45c; Andrejs Zemdega 95r.

All other images © Dorling Kindersley
For further information see:
www.dkimages.com